Help Your Child

Read and Succeed

Help Your Child

Read and Succeed

A Parents' Guide

Carl B. Smith, Ph.D.

GRAYSON BERNARD
PUBLISHERS

Book design by Kathleen McConahay
Illustrations by Addie Seabarkrob
Cover design by Addie Seabarkrob
Cover photograph by Alan Sinn

Publisher's Cataloging in Publication
(Prepared by Quality Books Inc.)

Smith, Carl Bernard, 1932-
    Help your child read and succeed: a parents' guide /
Carl B. Smith, Ph.D. --
    p. cm.
    ISBN 0-9628556-1-8

    1. Reading -- Parent participation.   I. Title

LB1050   372.4   91-73118

Grayson Bernard Publishers
223 S. Pete Ellis Dr., Suite 12
Bloomington, Indiana 47408

Dedication

For Ginny, who is always teaching me something new about parenting.

Contents

Foreword

Can you make a difference in your child's success in school? Oh yes, an enormous difference; especially where learning to read is concerned. Study after study confirms the importance of what the parent does beginning in early childhood and continuing through the school years. Parents who read with their children, give them books, ask them stimulating questions, and offer them hints on how to understand text, give their children a big boost toward success. This book helps parents in their important role as their children's most powerful guide to reading and learning. It contains directions, guidelines and activities to build a positive environment and a relationship that promotes learning. Here, the parent is as much the learner as the child. Together they grow and learn how to use reading in school and outside.

Acknowledgments

My four children, Madonna, Anthony, Regina, and Marla, gave me the interest and the practice I needed to turn my professional and personal interests toward parent education. Of course I had considerable help in preparing this book. Steve Gottleib collected information and edited early drafts of this work. Susan Yerolemou shepherded all of the people at Grayson Bernard to keep our project moving. Frances Weinstein used her library experience to build several booklists to guide parents. Eugene Reade performed his usual careful proofreading that always turns into another edit. Kathleen McConahay kept asking questions and pushing for helpful appendices. And Addie Seabarkrob created the wonderful illustrations for this book. I acknowledge my debt of gratitude to all these people with whom I have the pleasure of working.

Introduction

Reading involves more than simply looking at words on the printed page; it is an active, creative process of communication between the writer and reader. As you work to help your child, it's essential that you emphasize that the main point of reading is to get meaning. Even though we will work on various things from vocabulary development to study skills, our goal is always to build a message in the mind of the reader.

This book is based on the simple idea that a child will be more successful if he feels that he's making progress. As a parent, you are in the best position to promote this sense of success. First of all, your child trusts and looks up to you, and wants to please you. In addition, you can work with your child in the comfortable, familiar surroundings of your own home, where the pressures of getting good grades and of competing with other students are not present. You are ideally situated to encourage your child's successes, and to help him work through areas of difficulty.

You'll find that many examples are used in this book. This is by design; the examples, exercises and diagrams are meant to help you and your child understand what the text is explaining. We encourage you to use plenty of examples yourself, so that your child can follow your meaning as well.

Some of the suggestions and exercises in this book may seem obvious to you. Please recall that you have developed your own reading skills over a number of years. Many of the techniques that you apply as you read have become second nature, but you had to learn those skills at some point. Your child is learning them now, so don't pass up the opportunity to help teach him when it seems appropriate.

This book is not meant to replace school learning. Rather, it's designed to supplement the work that your child is doing in school, and to focus on specific skills and strategies that fit a parent-child relationship. The book can also help you understand what is involved in your child's classroom reading instruction, and what you can do to enhance that instruction.

Each of the chapters in this book contains a wealth of information on reading and on how your child can progress in reading with your guidance.

Chapter One addresses the parent's role and reviews some of the mental processes involved in reading.

Chapter Two provides many suggestions on reading materials for children, and discusses how your child's interests, motivations and attitudes can affect his progress in reading and learning.

In the third chapter, you'll discover how to help your child set a purpose for reading, and how the child can deal with new words and with complex text.

Vocabulary is discussed in Chapter Four, as are some basic phonics rules. At the end of that chapter, you'll find exercises designed to emphasize these skills.

Chapter Five underscores the value of learning a reading vocabulary, synonyms, antonyms and homonyms. Vocabulary building activities are included.

In Chapter Six you'll see why your reading aloud is so important to your child's reading development.

Chapter Seven discusses reading for information,

reading maps, charts and graphs.

Ideas on how to select books for children are provided in Chapter Eight. Examples of these books are given, along with several topic areas for parents to explore.

"Flexibility and Reading Speed" is the title of Chapter Nine. In that section, we explain the PARS study-reading method, and introduce speed reading and skimming.

Chapter Ten reviews the parent's role and approaches to helping children learn to read.

Helping your child learn to read can be a rewarding experience for both of you. In working with your child, you'll be offering him an opportunity to develop skills that he will be using throughout his life. At the same time, you'll be learning, too. You will discover your child's abilities, his strengths and weaknesses, and his interests. Don't be surprised if you end up learning some things about yourself: how good a teacher you are, how patient, and how supportive. You may even find that the shared experience has brought the two of you closer together.

Chapter One

Helping children with reading and learning

The object of teaching a child is to enable him to get along without his teacher.
—Elbert Green Hubbard

A s a child starts school, he or she expects to learn to read. More than a few children come home after the first day of school and complain that they haven't learned to read yet. Actually a beginning kindergartner already knows a lot about reading. Recent research shows that reading and writing begin long before a child reaches the first grade. A child picks up cues from television, from other print media, from signs, and from his parents. Together, these and other factors affect the learner's attitude and sense of direction regarding what kind of reader and writer he will be.

In these early years, teachers and parents need to help children develop a desire to learn and a curiosity about the printed word. This will help children develop a strong interest in books and an enthusiasm for learning.

These early experiences will shape your child's opinion of reading. If he feels good about his progress, he's likely to stick with reading and continue to improve. On the other hand, if his first reading experiences are negative, he may avoid books altogether.

In your role as a parent, you're in a position to help your child overcome some of the hurdles which a young learner may face. By offering your support and guidance, you can enable him to move ahead in reading instead of allowing early problems to multiply. The more you can do to make reading interesting and meaningful, the more likely your child is to succeed in school.

Scribbles have meaning

In the early years of your child's life there are some guidelines that you can follow to make reading and learning important.

➡ **Let your child see you read.** As your child's first and most influential model, you show the value of reading by reading in his or her presence. Gradually a message is impressed on your child's brain: "Reading is important because mom and dad do it regularly."

➡ **Read to your child.** By reading to your child, you let him know that reading is a personal communication. It is a warm, friendly experience. In the early months, merely reading the newspaper aloud with your child on your lap or lying next to you begins a relationship that grows across the years as you read children's easy books, fairy tales, adventure stories, information books. Some parents make bedtime reading a nightly ritual that lasts many years.

➡ Listen and respond to your child's questions.
We all know that young children can drive us crazy with questions that seem like childish prattle. They ask questions in order to learn. We parents should treat them as opportunities to learn as well. Many of our children's questions we can answer from our own background, but some may stump us. Those are the ones that enable us to go to a book, or the encyclopedia, and find an answer by reading. Isn't that another important image you want to place in your child's mind —"We can find answers in books."?

➡ Encourage your child to write — and then ask for the meaning of the message. During the first couple of grades in school, children learn to print, to spell, and to write messages that we can understand. But those messages are usually brief, and so it is quite normal for a parent to ask: "Will you tell me more about this message or story?" That gives a child a chance to explain what is actually on his mind. Even in preschool years, however, most children scribble and draw on paper. Sometimes those scribbles contain random letters of the alphabet. Researchers have learned that these scribbles have meaning in the minds of the children who write them. Children realize the printed page stands for a story or a message and they often have a story in mind when they scribble and draw. It helps, therefore, for you to ask about those scribbles by saying: "Tell me what you are writing."

➡ Build a reading environment in your house.
Place books, magazines, and newspapers in prominent places and encourage everyone to use them—in the bathroom or next to a favorite chair. Read to each other; write to each other, even if it's only a note on the refrigerator. Through these various activities you create the positive attitude that reading and writing are useful, fun, and important. That's a winning attitude for school.

The parent as tutor

The classroom teacher's role is to decide how to approach reading instruction and to choose the reading materials that the students will use. Parents play a complementary role as a tutor at home. To help your child apply what he's learning in school to reading and writing in the real world, you should constantly let him know that he can learn to read *successfully*. You can show your child that he can use the skills he's learning in the classroom by reading magazines, newspapers, and books at home.

How is the work I do with my child at home different from the reading practice he gets in school?

At home, you and your child can work on reading at a pace and in a setting which are comfortable for the two of you. Is a card table fun? Is there a blackboard in the kitchen? Can you sit on a porch swing and concentrate? You can focus strictly on those areas that you think are important for your child to understand.

Just as a tutor helps focus learning, explains ideas that are not clear to the learner, and provides guided practice, so can you do those things for your child at home. Without focus, your child doesn't know what he's trying to achieve. Thus when your child brings home a reading assignment, act your role as a friendly tutor by following these directions:

➡ **Help focus the activity.** What is the purpose? What do you want to learn?

➡ **Keep the learner on target.** Are you achieving the purpose? Are you learning anything yet?

➡ **Answer your child's questions.** Try to clarify directions or language when they pose a stumbling block.

➡ **Practice reading together.** Use the assignment as an opportunity to read together, to learn together. Ask your child to read to you and be willing to read to him.

Creating a positive environment

As you give your child reading practice at home, you promote learning simply by offering a place to learn that's free of the competitive pressures of the classroom. The home setting is ideal for letting your child know that he's making good progress: that his answers are good, that his ideas are interesting or that you know he is working and you appreciate his hard work. If you give your child this kind of feedback, he's likely to feel better about his reading achievements, and he may be more willing to tackle even tougher exercises.

How can I be sure my child experiences success?

In offering your child a taste of success, it's important to begin with exercises that are within his abilities. As the exercises get a bit harder, it's important that you continue to provide encouragement. In periods of slower progress, be sure to tell him that the exercise he's working on really *is* a tough one, that he's making a good effort, and that he's going to figure out the answer by continuing to work on the exercise.

Creating a positive environment means more than encouraging your child with compliments about his

efforts. He also needs to see that he is making progress and has some resources to do his school work. Helping your child make progress in reading is what this book is all about.

Just as a coach builds team spirit, creates incentives, and works to get his players good equipment and facilities, so does a parent who wants his child to succeed. Your child needs to feel that his efforts on reading and learning are important in the family, and he senses this importance through your concern and through your enthusiasm for his accomplishments.

One of his incentives for hard work is the chance to show what he can do. Listen to him read. Ask him to retell a story. When he has written a summary to a story or a reaction to it, read his paper aloud and discuss his ideas with pride. He worked hard; now is his time to be a star. To make homework more valuable in his eyes, supply him with his own desk or workspace with dictionary, paper, pens — and maybe access to a computer, if that's within your means. If not, young children are also fascinated with using typewriters.

By creating this kind of positive environment you are setting a positive tone for success. Hard work, of course, is still an essential ingredient.

Your child may get impatient with his reading efforts and decide that it just isn't worth the trouble to keep trying. This is a natural reaction, but it is one that you can and should try to overcome. You are an important role model. If you can show your child that you value your own education, then he is likely to adopt the same view of learning. Reading and doing well in school will take on new meaning in the child's mind.

The reading process: Building meaning

Before looking at specific techniques to help your child, you need to ask yourself what reading means to you. In this book the term *reading* does not mean merely pronouncing words or searching the page for specific facts. Reading here means a search for meaning — and that's much more complicated and important than learning to decode (sound out) word by word. Decoding (*phonics*) is only one of many tools that a reader uses to build meaning —that is, *to read.*

To get a sense of what reading is, think about what you have done so far in this book. You chose to examine this book because you are interested in your child's welfare. You want him or her to succeed in school and in life. You know that reading ability is probably the most valuable skill a person has in his search for school knowledge and in continued learning on the job. You know that those who do not read well often become problems in school, often are unemployed, and therefore cannot live satisfactory lives in our knowledge-based society. For those reasons, you want to help your child hone his reading ability to its highest level. In other words, you are interested and motivated. You think you can make a difference, and you are entirely correct. No one is more important to your child's success in reading than you are.

Once the topic of this book drew you inside its pages, you wanted to see if the contents and the style suited your purposes. You may have reviewed the table of contents or the introduction where sections of the book are summarized briefly. Depending on your child's immediate needs, you may have turned to a specific section — vocabulary building, for instance. You may have asked: "How do I know if my child's vocabulary is satisfactory for the reading he has to do? I'll read this chapter to find vocabulary building ideas." Thus you set a purpose or began to ask yourself questions that you wanted answered.

As you move through a chapter in this book, you have a sense of whether or not you are getting helpful answers to your questions or are building a meaning that suits your purpose. As you read, new questions or different purposes begin to surface. Then you start to

monitor your comprehension anew. You keep asking in the back of your head if you are learning anything helpful. If you are not, you adjust; that is, you reread, you look ahead, you stop and reflect, you look up definitions, and so on. As a mature reader, you regularly monitor your progress towards building meaning.

When you are finished with a section, you may ask yourself: "Now what do I know? What is useful here? How am I different? Am I better prepared to help my child with her reading? Did this book offer helpful resources for parents?" And even though you may not ask questions and summarize consciously, as an efficient reader you perform those functions.

That's what effective reading is — a thinking process that starts with interest and purpose, works to build meaning, and changes the individual's mind or feelings. That's the long range sense of reading you want to communicate to your child.

The mature reader has already mastered the complex process of reading. He understands that reading is a search for meaning, and that the main purpose of reading is to get or build a message. Because the skills of reading have become second nature to the experienced reader, it's sometimes difficult to step back and figure out what it takes for a young person to learn how to deal with the printed page and how to construct a message in the mind. We will discuss some of the things a reader's mind can do as it builds meaning.

To start with, it's very helpful for you and your child to start from the idea that the reader and the writer are engaged in a kind of conversation. Although it's not the same as a face-to-face talk, both the reader and the writer bring ideas to their "meeting" that are very important. The writer starts the process by posing the topic and generating a certain direction of thought. However, the reader will be able to make sense of the message only if he also brings background and thoughts to the message. If the writer and reader don't share enough mutual ideas, there is no communication. In the end, it will be the reader who constructs meaning based on his interaction with the writer. With that in mind, let's find ways for you to help your child engage in this complex interaction.

Are there clues that can help my child get meaning from what he reads?

Before, during, and after reading

When people make love, they don't stop to think about the stages of lovemaking. It all blends together in one continuous experience. It's only when psychologists step back to analyze the experience that they break it up into foreplay, intercourse, and afterglow. In order to talk about lovemaking and to make it more understandable, they label different aspects of what is, in fact, an integrated experience. A similar thing happens in discussing reading.

To make reading more explainable, we talk about before, during, and after reading, even though the act of reading is an integrated experience. By looking at different aspects of reading, we hope to improve its teaching and learning. The outline and explanations that follow remind us of the important aspects of reading as a meaning-building process. They help us focus on skills and strategies that make us more effective. But we certainly don't want to make the mistake of confusing some of these skills and strategies with the total act of reading.

You may feel that this discussion is more for psy-

READING: BUILDING MEANING

BEFORE READING
- ➠ Find mutual ground with the author
- ➠ Search background for ideas/vocabulary
- ➠ Set a purpose

DURING READING
- ➠ Ask questions
- ➠ Monitor understanding
- ➠ Adjust thinking

AFTER READING
- ➠ Summarize ideas
- ➠ Apply the experience

---

chologists than it is for parents. You may want to get to the practical stuff that will make your child a better reader. We will do that shortly, but this overview of the reading process helps you establish a valuable perspective: *the reader builds meaning.* The reader doesn't soak up meaning. The reader must act vigorously to construct a meaning from the text he is reading. All the other things that you do to help your child have the purpose of helping him work with the printed page in order to build meaning. Unless that focus on constructing meaning is maintained, the other activities may become distractions instead of aids. So let's review briefly the headings that appear in the outline.

Before reading

Think of this as a warm-up period, a time of mental preparation. Just as the athlete stretches to get ready for a game, so a reader looks at a book or chapter, asks himself what he knows and whether he and the author are on the same wavelength. You can help your child approach a new article by suggesting he flip through the pages to see what ideas pop up; to see if the vocabulary seems familiar; to make associations with past experiences; to try to stimulate questions that he wants to be answering. That kind of preparation may lead to a sense of purpose for reading the article. It is quite helpful, then, for you to ask: "What would you like to get out of this article?" "What purpose can you set for yourself?"

Don't be afraid to spend time discussing your child's preliminary ideas or some vocabulary that bothers him. Recent research has reinforced the value of these stretching exercises, this time to focus on the type of selection, on the vocabulary, on the reasons for reading. And by taking time to preview the selection, you emphasize the importance of reading as an exercise in building meaning.

During reading

In the past we may have thought of reading as a passive activity. One boy told us that when he reads, his "brain soaks up the page." Now we know that the good reader actively pursues reading. He wrestles the ideas to the ground and struggles to make them manageable. You can help your child during reading by reminding him to keep searching for answers to his early questions and to his purpose. "Are you finding your answers? Are you making sense of this article?" If he is not making sense, ask him what he needs to do to get on track. Should he look ahead to make better predictions? Should he review what he's already read with a different purpose? Would it help if he looked up a couple of key words (or discussed them with you)? By asking those questions, you remind your child that a good reader is flexible and is always thinking. It is quite appropriate to change perspectives and to rethink the ideas in his active struggle to build meaning.

After reading

At the end of the day some people take a moment to ask themselves: "What does this day mean to me? What value does it have?" After cleaning the house or finishing a project at work, don't you step back for a moment to relish the way it looks or to think what the project means for your company or for you? Reading is like that, too. When your child comes to the end of the page or chapter or book, you want him to admire what he's done and to see where the ideas will help him. You can aid that process by asking questions like:

➠ **Did you like this story?**
➠ **What seemed most important to you?**
➠ **Is this story like any other story you have read?**
➠ **Are there some parts that you want to share with me?**
➠ **How can you use these ideas (experiences)?**

Through this kind of follow-up discussion, you encourage your child to consolidate his reading experience and to put some finishing touches on the meaning he has built.

Skills and meaning

The most important thing you can do to help your child is to keep him focused on meaning. It's like keeping your mind set on winning the game in sports. In the middle of a basketball game, you don't distract yourself by wondering if you are dribbling the ball correctly. Instead, you work intensely to win the game. During practice sessions you can ask yourself what you have to do to improve your dribbling or passing or foul shooting.

So, too, in reading you want to keep pursuing the meaning: "Does this make sense to me? What can I do to get it to make sense to me?"

Just as a basketball player has to have skills in order to win the game, a reader has to have skills in order to make sense of the printed page. You should assume that those skills are taught in school and are practiced there. They are of course practiced whenever one reads. But you may want to help your son or daughter with some of the more important skills when questions arise as you are reading together. Those important skills are *decoding, seeing relationships*, and *evaluating*.

Decoding

Decoding (phonics) is an obvious and a basic skill for reading. After all, the alphabet is a print code for speech sounds—though not a perfect one. In your role as a gentle tutor, you can be most effective by keeping the big picture. If your child stumbles over a word or asks for help in pronouncing it, use the following pattern of questions to help:

➠ **What word makes sense there?**

➠ **What word begins with the same sound as the one in the book?**

➠ **Do you see any phonics patterns (spelling patterns) in the word that could help you in getting the word? That means, can you sound it out?**

If you keep asking that series of questions, you help your child approach a decoding problem with the idea that its purpose is to make sense. And if he still doesn't come up with the correct word, tell him what it is and move on. If you notice that the decoding problems are numerous, alert your child's teacher. All it takes is a note or a quick telephone call. Maybe the teacher will ask you to help your child with some material that she sends home for practice. There are some practice activities later in this book that may serve you and your child, also.

Seeing relationships

Another major reading skill that aids comprehension is that of making connections among ideas, of seeing relationships. It is this skill that enables a person to draw conclusions, make comparisons, and find a generalization about a series of events or ideas. A person displays this skill in responding to questions, such as:

➠ **What is this all about? (What is the theme?)**

➠ **Is this story like any other story you have read?**

➠ **After reading that article, what conclusions do you draw?**

➠ **What is the main argument she is using?**

➠ **What do you think the main character will do next?**

You should assume, of course, that the teacher in school is working regularly on developing the skill of seeing relationships. You can promote the use of that skill through the kinds of questions that you ask your child. Seeing relationships may take much time and practice for a child to achieve. Give him a chance to develop this thinking skill. Once again, if you are concerned that your child does not know how to discuss questions like those listed above, draw the teacher's attention to his need. She may set up a practice program in which you can be of assistance.

Later in this book there are practice exercises that work on relationship skills.

Evaluating

"Is that movie any good? Would you recommend that book? Why are you going to vote for that person?"

We respond to evaluation questions all the time. It is a natural part of our interaction with others to make judgments and to reflect positive and negative reactions to events in the world around us. We call that kind of thinking *critical thinking.*

As our children read, we want them to act like critical thinkers. They are accustomed to critical thinking in many aspects of their lives, and we want them to learn to think critically about their reading. Most children have heard their parents encourage them to watch some television programs and not to watch others. "Why don't you watch this *National Geographic* program on endangered animals. It will make us aware of how we can preserve nature." "That television show has too much violence in it. I do not want you to watch it." Behind our recommendations are judgments: preserving nature is good (OK to watch); excessive violence corrupts the mind (do not watch).

In our discussions over books and articles, then, we can prompt critical thinking (evaluation) by asking questions like these:

➠ *How is that information useful?*

➠ *Why did you like (not like) that part of the story?*

➠ *How could you change the story to get this character to act in an ethical way?*

➠ *Who else should read this? Why?*

Parent action

As you can see, the important skills listed above are not deep secrets hidden from everyone except the high priest of education. But for your child to use these skills easily and regularly, he has to have a lot of practice, as he would for any athletic skill. Though skills are taught in school, your child may not have sufficient practice opportunities there to make them second nature. That's where you can help. Keep your child reading for meaning, and guide his thinking by asking the kinds of questions that we have just discussed—not as a test, but as a way of learning and discussing things that interest you.

Chapter Two

Creating interest and positive attitudes

*Keep your face to the sunshine and you
cannot see the shadow.*
— Helen Keller

T o read well, your child has to pay attention to the text and concentrate on the message. If your child is easily distracted or doesn't listen closely to directions, she's not going to understand as much as a classmate who is better able to focus on the subject at hand. Interests and attitudes influence the things on which your child will concentrate. It is valuable, therefore, for you to take reasonable steps to examine ways that you can use her interests and can develop positive attitudes that will help her read, listen, and concentrate long enough to learn.

Concentration is not simply an act of the will that becomes powerful through practice. It is more than that. We know, for instance, that our concentration improves when we are interested in the topic. If we are interested in decorating our house, we can focus our attention on a magazine that features interior house designs. Our children are no different. That's the main reason we encourage parents to find books that interest their children. Then children are more likely to pay attention while reading. They are more likely to concentrate on what they are doing. Finding interests, then, is a good place to start.

Later in this chapter we will give more specific ideas on how to concentrate on school work. Those ideas include trying to fake an interest in the subject, writing notes to yourself about your reading, and summarizing or convincing someone else that the information you have just read is valuable or interesting. Some studies have shown that even when people do not start with an interest in a subject, they can become interested by acting as if they are interested. In a sense, they trick themselves into believing that they have an interest, and then they learn better because of it.

Developing an early interest in reading

Some interests seem to develop naturally, perhaps because they are somehow a part of our genetic code. Some people seem to have an inborn interest in active, physical subjects such as sports. Others seem to have an inborn propensity for reflective activities such as philosophizing or being a college professor. Then there are other interests that are learned or developed over time. Chidren may develop these interests by watching those around them, by competing in school, or by watching television. Likewise, a child may admire a person and then want to do the things that person does.

Since reading fluently means so much to school success and to job success, we want our children to see reading as one of their most valuable tools. That is an attitude, of course, but the attitude can be built only if we can get our children interested in reading in the first place. In other words, we have to help them develop an interest in reading, whether they have an inborn affinity for it or not. Besides that, we also hope that our children will find pleasure and learn about life through reading. That's another reason why we want to start as early as possible to build an interest in this essential tool.

Preschool books

By reading to a preschool-age child from books with colorful pictures, simple stories and predictable sentences, you can help her develop an early interest in books and the habit of reading along with you. Appendix A lists books that can be read to your preschooler. Many of these titles are old standbys; some are more recent. Most are probably available at your local library and your bookstore.

Read-aloud books

Even after your child learns to read, she will still enjoy hearing you tell a good story. Learn to use your own excitement for stories by reading them aloud. If you can't build up enthusiasm for the book, don't read it or you will kill the book for your child. You promote interest through your own fondness for children's stories or through your own enthusiasm. Reading aloud can promote a positive attitude toward reading and increase the child's interest in language. In Chapter Six you will find lists of read-aloud books intended for children ages three and up, and these can be used to supplement the earlier group of titles intended for preschoolers. But please remember that the ages are merely approximations. Try a few books with your child and find her comfort level.

Predictable books

One very good way to help your young reader is to read from books with predictable story lines. In such stories as "The House that Jack Built," your child is likely to grasp the repetitive "plot" before very many verses are read.

This is the House that Jack Built.

This is the mat that lay in the House that Jack Built.

This is the rat, that ate the mat that lay in the House that Jack Built.

This is the cat, that killed the rat, that ate the mat that lay in the House that Jack Built.

This is the dog, that worried the cat, that killed the rat, that ate the mat that lay in the House that Jack Built.

Even if you don't have access to such books, there's no limit to the number of stories of this kind that you and your child could make up:

A mouse was walking through the woods one day. Suddenly he fell in a mud puddle and couldn't get out.

A rabbit came along and tried to help the mouse get out. But the rabbit fell in the mud and couldn't get out.

A fox came along and tried to help the mouse and the rabbit. But the fox fell in the mud and couldn't get out.

A deer came along. . .

Stories of this kind can go on with more animals of ever-increasing size until the skunk comes along and the pattern reverses itself because everyone wants to escape the smell. Let your child join in the "refrain" and suggest animals of her own, dragging elephants, giraffes and dinosaurs into the crowded mud puddle.

These predictable, repetitive stories are best when accompanied by attractive illustrations. They also may include rhyme or rhythmic language that children can chant. Here are a few predictable books for five-, six-, and seven-year olds to read on their own or perhaps with a little help from you. If needed, these titles can supply extra reading practice for second or third graders.

Barohas, Sarah E. *I Was Walking Down the Road.*
Brown, Marcia. *The Three Billy Goats Gruff.*
Eastman, P.D. *Are You My Mother?*
Fox, Mem. *Hattie and the Fox.*
Galdone, Paul. *The Three Little Pigs.*
Galdone, Paul. *Henny Penny.*
Hawkins, Colin and Jacqui. *Old Mother Hubbard.*
Hutchins, Pat. *Good-Night Owl.*
Langstaff, John. *Frog Went A-Courtin'.*
Martin, Bill Jr. *Brown, Brown Bear, What Do You See?*
Preston, Edna Mitchell. *Where Did My Mother Go?*
Sendak, Maurice. *Where the Wild Things Are.*
Zaid, Barry. *Chicken Little.*

An additional list of predictable books can be found in Appendix B.

The "language story" approach

Children love to tell the same story over and over, and they get great pleasure from making up their own stories. This interest in stories can be used to motivate them to read. More importantly, it can be used to help children understand the link between speech and written words. This is known as the "language story" technique. It involves having your child tell a story she has made up herself, and then your writing it for her so she can reread it. The child's own language is used to write "the story." The impression that this creates in the mind of the child follows this logic:

- What I can think, I can say.
- What I can say can be written down, so others can read it.
- What others can read, I can read.

Here is a sample language story dictated by a six year old.

Our Hamster

We have a hamster in our room.
Her name is Miss Lori Blackberry.
She lives in a cage.
She likes to roam around the room.
We like our hamster.

Because these stories are usually very short, the child can remember most of what she said even if she can't figure out all of the words if written elsewhere. In being able to read her own story, she experiences success and learns a valuable lesson about the link between ideas, speech and print. Using her own story, you can even help your child discover various punctuation marks, for example, that the "?" means a question is being asked; that s after the word *bird* means there's more than one; and so on. That experience will help her understand stories written by other people.

Language Story Directions

This is a very informal technique for keeping the reader's interest high and for showing her the relation between her own speech and the written word. Keep it all informal and relaxed.

- Get a large sheet of paper or a large tablet on which you will print the story.
- Ask your child to tell any short story, including something that happened to her that day—at school, at play, while watching TV.
- As your child tells her story, print it on the sheet of paper. If you can, begin each sentence on a new line. Write the story as closely as you can to the language of the child.
- Try to keep the story fairly short. One page of print is usually enough.
- When finished writing, ask your child to read it back to you. It doesn't matter if she gets all the words exactly as she said them. You want her to get the basic association between speech and print. Feel free to get her back on track if she starts wandering too far away from the original text. But once she picks up the tempo of her own language, let her continue.
- After your child has reread the story several times and seems to know it by heart, you may want to cut the paper up into sentence strips and let her put the story back together by arranging the sentence strips in order. By doing that, you are helping her get closer and closer to a specific identification of the whole message with the actual words that make it up.
- Some children would enjoy drawing a picture to illustrate the story they have told.

Even for older children, nothing works as well in getting across the link between speech and print as having a child read back what she has just spoken. A reluctant reader's attitude may begin to change as she

What can I do to use my child's own interests to improve reading?

sees her words become real (it's right there in print) and valuable (other people are interested in what she has "written").

By the age of six, a child learns to recognize a large number of spoken words, perhaps as many as twenty thousand different forms. This background in spoken language can help your child develop her abilities in reading and using the printed word. The big advantage of the language story approach is that it builds on something your child can already do successfully: express herself through language. Using the language story approach is like telling your child: "Your language is good. Start with it and learn how to develop it."

Encouraging new interests

Everyone prefers to spend time doing things that are interesting, and children are no different. You already know many of the things your child likes just by listening. Simply talking or answering questions about things seen on television can give you an idea of what interests your child — animals, cartoon characters, space science, mystery stories, and so on.

Obviously, the best way to discover your child's interests is to talk with her and listen closely to what she says. Bring home books from your library or point out newspaper articles about those subjects that your child has mentioned. Show her some pictures, let her pick some that appeal to her, and have her make up a story about one or more of them.

If your daughter brings a rock or leaf to show you, let her explain how and where she found it, why she picked it up, what else she would like to know. These daily opportunities not only reveal your child's interests but also give you chances to suggest books and magazines for further exploration.

Don't forget to offer some small reward or sign of

recognition when your child has done something that marks a step forward in the process of learning to read. This could be anything from posting a congratulations card on the refrigerator for the whole family to see, to bringing home a new book. Sometimes, as simple a gesture as a pat on the head or words of praise from you can mean more than any prize.

The reason you want to discover new interests is to open up a broad world of reading. When you say: "I heard you talk about Teenage Mutant Ninja Turtles and so I brought you one of their comic books," you show that your child's interests are important to you and that books can match almost any interest. Those moments open other windows. "Do you know whom the Ninja Turtles are named after? Famous artists. We could get a book in the library and see what Leonardo and his friends painted."

In reviewing interests and trying to find new ones, it might help you to keep a list so you can bring books and newspapers to your child. The Interest Inventory which follows may also help. Feel free to add your own questions.

If your child is able to read the inventory, let her fill it out by herself. If not, read it to her. Tell her that this information will help you and her find books and entertainment that you can share. Show your child that her interests are important by getting one book immediately, one that matches a topic that your child checked "Like a Lot."

Increasing attention span

It may frustrate a parent to see that a child who doesn't pay attention in school can spend a whole day playing Nintendo or watching television. Not surprisingly, the more interest a child has in an activity, the more time she is able to concentrate on it. If you plan reading activities around your child's interests, she is more likely to stay involved with what is being read. In

INTEREST INVENTORY

After school I like to _____ .

My favorite TV programs are _____ .

My favorite game is_____ .

My favorite subject is _____ .

My favorite sport is _____ .

My hobby is _____ .

What do you like to read about? Put a check mark in the column that shows how you like each topic.

	DON'T LIKE	LIKE A LITTLE	LIKE A LOT
Stories about real animals	_____	_____	_____
Mystery stories	_____	_____	_____
Adventure stories	_____	_____	_____
Funny stories	_____	_____	_____
Comic books	_____	_____	_____
Science fiction	_____	_____	_____
Jack and the Bean Stalk	_____	_____	_____
The Three Billy Goats Gruff	_____	_____	_____
Cinderella	_____	_____	_____
Drawing, painting, coloring	_____	_____	_____
Cutting and pasting	_____	_____	_____
Doing puppet shows	_____	_____	_____
Making model cars	_____	_____	_____
Taking pictures	_____	_____	_____
Sewing, cooking	_____	_____	_____
Doing science experiments	_____	_____	_____

order to become a reader your child needs to read a lot, just as she would have to play a lot to become a smooth tennis player. Therefore, you want to find ways to *gradually* expand the amount of time she spends on reading. Here are a few suggestions for holding your child's interest.

➡ **Vary the type of activity.** It's a good idea to plan several different kinds of exercises for a single session of reading practice. This is especially important for a child who is having trouble grasping an idea, because she then has to be kept interested longer than a child who catches on right away. Although all the exercises in one homework session may focus on a particular story, you can introduce it in a number of ways: for example, through reading part of it aloud, then discussing one of the ideas or predicting what will happen, or game-playing, or writing. Here is an example of how you might set up a practice session:

Parent: *"This story shows how children find a secret passageway into a land of strange creatures. To get started, why don't I read a page aloud, then you read a page."*
(Parent reads)
(Child reads)

Parent: *"What do you think will happen next?"*

Parent and child discuss briefly: Ideas will vary, of course.

Parent: *"Now you read the next 2-3 pages silently and then tell me what happened."*

You can see the pattern that is developing. First you help your child focus on the story by being a companion in the reading. Second, you show how to get started and to create questions that will give her purpose, particularly over a short time span. Third, you ask her to report to you what she is learning. When she reports or summarizes the two or three pages you asked her to read, praise her for sticking to the job and repeat the pattern. Don't wear out your child. If she seems eager to pursue the rest of the story on her own, ask her to read a couple of pages and report back. Keep your child predicting what will happen in the next event and then telling you the results of her prediction.

Don't be afraid to pick up the story with your child and read another page aloud, having her read aloud and then another couple of pages of silent reading. Gradually, over a period of months this routine will help most children improve their attention span during reading. This is because the pattern helps the reader focus and set questions for reading, and shows that reading can be managed in chunks. You don't have to do the whole thing in one sitting. You read a chunk to get its meaning and then read another chunk. When you need a break, you take it and then return to read another chunk. And so on.

In preparing practice sessions, you can make use of exercises such as the one just described, those explained in later chapters, or you can make up some of your own, according to the needs of your child.

➡ **Use information from the Interest Inventory to choose books your child will enjoy reading.** Whether your child is interested in mystery stories or books about far-off planets, it helps to place books and magazines around the house on those subjects of interest. Even if a book is too tough for your son or daughter to read alone, you can read it aloud and have the child read along with you. It's especially important for your child to realize that reading can be done for the sheer enjoyment of a good story, or to learn about something of personal interest, and not just because "the teacher says we have to read this." Chapter Eight includes some suggestions on choosing books that are best suited for your child.

➡ **Build activities around stories your child writes.** Writing is a natural ally to reading. Try to use

writing as a way to promote thinking and as a way to make reading more interesting. Your child's writing will probably be similar to the way she talks, so it should be easier for her to read her own words. Encourage her to write about the stories she reads or to write the kind of story she finds interesting. Your young author might even come up with pictures and captions, if she likes to draw or use a camera. Have your child write about your last trip, or the plot of a television show that you watched. If yours is a very young child, let her tell the story orally; you can then help write it down and your child can then read back what she said. See our previous discussion on "language stories." (page 21)

As much as possible, encourage your child to write about books she reads, things she learns, and questions she wants answered. Writing supports reading and is an excellent way to learn.

➡ **Use games to make practice sessions lively.**
Games involving the matching of words with pictures
are good practice for a child who's learning to read.
Matching sentences and pictures from inexpensive
books extends that idea. After you have read a story to
your child a number of times, you may want to cut the
pictures from the text to challenge your child to as-
semble the story as it occurred in the book. Under-
standably, you would do this kind of exercise with
"throwaway books," not with those that you want to
keep in your child's permanent library.

How can I build attitudes that will help promote reading?

Chapter Five suggests some common
games (such as Bingo) and simple activities (such as making paper cutouts)
that can be adapted to help your child
develop word skills. By combining reading practice with related activities, you
may be surprised to find that your child's
attention span can gradually increase.
When your child sees that reading and doing things
can go hand-in-hand, she will pay more attention and
over time develop the habit of sticking with reading.
But please remember, reading activities have to make
sense to your child. We use games to make reading fun
and sensible.

Motivating positive attitudes

Motivation is the persuasive power that prompts us to
act. We may be motivated to do something out of a
need to satisfy curiosity, explore new interests, reach
some goal, or simply to take part in an activity that
holds our attention. Not all motivation comes from
within us. It can come from outside as well: the need to
pass a test, for example, or to avoid possible harm by
not walking down a dark alley at night.
Motivating forces play a powerful role in the reading
process. Your child may feel outside pressure with
regard to schoolwork ("I have to get a passing grade,"

or "I have to do it because the teacher says so.") These are normal external pressures but need to be balanced with personal or intrinsic reasons to act. If your child feels these outside pressures are the only reasons for reading, she may begin to view reading as a chore, as something one has to do. You can expand her vision by focusing on her interests and by stressing that reading is rewarding on its own terms, not just something that must be done to meet a school requirement. Naturally, you want your child to see reading a book as a positive experience, both for learning and for pleasure.

The main reason we all are concerned about motivation is that motivation gives us the energy to work long enough to develop positive attitudes. Attitudes, that is, habits of the mind, guide our actions. If your child says: "When I need information, a book is a good place to look," she has a good attitude about reading for information. You can help build these positive attitudes by what you yourself say and do.

Motivation helps understanding because motivation involves purpose and energy. Without purpose and energy,

> **The best defense against a negative attitude is to make sure that it doesn't appear in the first place.**

your child will not comprehend a book. Her attitude can be positive or negative, strong or weak, but attitudes themselves do not determine whether or not she reads well. Your child may be strongly motivated to read a certain book because it discusses a subject of great interest to her. If the material is badly written, however, or is beyond your child's ability to understand, she may develop a negative attitude toward the book. If that negative experience happens often enough, she may begin to reject reading itself; it just isn't worth the pain to struggle with dull or difficult material.

You want your child to have a positive attitude, a

good feeling about reading. Those good feelings result from previous successes or from the fun promised by listening to Daddy read or from the warmth of being close to Mommy when she reads. They also result from the fun that a reader experiences from certain types of books. That fun explains why certain types of books hook their readers into reading the entire series, like the Hardy Boys or Nancy Drew. (Yes, they are still popular.) The Baby Sitters Club, Sweet Valley series, and books like *Amelia Bedelia* all fall into the same category—fun books that have their familiar characters acting out their familiar brand of humor and adventure. Just as adults return to Harlequin romances, western adventures, and spy thrillers, so do children appreciate their own series for their own reasons. In serial books, the child's interest and a sense of affinity for the characters work together to keep her coming back for each new book in the series.

Once after a six year old had been in first grade for two weeks I asked her what she now thought about school. "I like it a little," she said, "but I still hate it a lot." That attitude reflects what she thought her parents or her friends expected her to say. After two weeks in school, she would not on her own say, "I still hate it a lot." Attitudes stem from many sources, especially from the home and the neighborhood. That little six year old already carried a negative attitude about school—an attitude that will influence her performance, no matter what the teacher does. Notice that she had to say that she hated it even though there were some things happening that she evidently liked—"I like it a little."

Attitudes about reading can be formed in the same way. After repeated negative statements at home or in the neighborhood, it is very difficult for a young child to believe that reading will benefit her. Teachers try to counteract negative attitudes by relying heavily on motivational techniques. If a child is exposed only to materials she feels are dull, outside her interest, or beyond her understanding, she'll develop a negative attitude toward reading. With the enormous number and variety of children's books available today, there's no reason for this to happen to your child.

Very young children are attracted to books with plenty of colorful pictures. With such books you can show your child the excitement of words and pictures. Children love to find details in pictures. An older child may get caught up in mystery stories, science fiction, westerns, sports stories, dinosaurs, or King Arthur. Once hooked, children find that books can fill areas of their interest, and a positive attitude toward reading grows naturally. By paying attention to your child's likes and dislikes, you can help build positive attitudes.

Steps for developing attitudes

The way we develop attitudes can be broken down into these steps:

Steps for Building Attitudes

1. Become aware that positive attitudes exist. (Some people like to read.)

2. Respond to someone's action that shows the attitude. ("I see you like to read and it makes you happy.")

3. Value an activity and talk about liking it. ("I see John reading and enjoying mystery stories. That's good and I like to read them, too.")

4. Make a place in your life for the activity you value. ("For at least twenty minutes every night, I will read a book I enjoy.")

What do these steps mean to you as you try to help your child improve? First of all, it means that you have to see yourself in those four steps. Are you at step number four where you are willing to make a place in your life for working on reading on a regular basis? It doesn't have to be a burden. You can find ways of making it pleasant and rewarding. If nothing else, it is rewarding to know that you are giving your child the advantage of a positive attitude towards reading and school. But somehow you have to organize your schedule so you can invest twenty to thirty minutes each day to read and to study with your child.

You can use the four steps as a means for building mental habits in your child. Are there people in the family or in the neighborhood who exemplify the kinds of attitudes towards reading that you want your child to have? Point them out. Make her aware that many people read and are successful because of it. Whether these people read for fun or read for information, talk to your child about them. Don't forget yourself—you are the most important example your child will see. You can help by making reading a

significant part of your family's daily life. For example, you can read aloud the headlines from the morning paper, or spend time together in the evening taking turns reading from a book.

Second, praise people who show the attitude you are trying to develop. And ask your child to talk about an activity where the positive attitude reveals itself. Ask her about those children who read a lot or who seem to enjoy reading. What do they do? What do they believe about reading that enables them to read well or to enjoy reading? In this step you want your child to think about and to talk about the activity that reveals a desirable habit of mind. You might help at this point by bringing home books on subjects in which your child expressed an interest. ("You said you thought you might like to be a pilot someday. Here is a library book on some of the things that pilots do. See what you think.") You could then talk about receiving books. What does your activity enable your child to do? What does your activity say about your own thoughts? (It shows that you think books are important, but more to the point, it shows that you think your child is important.)

The third step is a big leap forward in attitude development. Now your child has to say that reading is valuable. Sometimes it takes a long time for children to arrive at this point, especially if they have few positive examples around them. Don't force this step. It has to arrive naturally. Remember that your child will value reading or will turn to reading for information or for pleasure when she sees that reading gives her something that she needs or wants. Sometimes that realization takes many years. For one of my children it didn't happen until he was in junior high school. You can help by repeating steps one and two, and especially by showing your own commitment to reading in your own life.

The fourth step is to show that you value an activity by making a regular place for it. Some people will say that reading for pleasure is a value or that it is valuable to learn to study-read effectively, but they do not put that value into practice. Some people, it seems, do not have enough sense of order about their lives to make a place for important activities or for activities they say are valuable. Instead, they let daily events take over their lives and can't seem to organize their priorities. Getting through the next day, whatever it may bring, seems to be the only priority they have.

One technique to help your child make a place for reading activities is called *visualizing*. When your child says that she values a certain kind of reading, ask her to picture herself doing that activity. She should make the picture as specific as possible—the place, the time, the lighting, the purpose for reading. Ask her to picture herself doing the reading and feeling the pleasure of completing the activity. For example, she will be confident in school; she will experience an adventure vicariously; she will be well read on the subject and can respond better than any of her friends, and so on. Also ask her to picture herself organizing her time so she will carry out that activity. Each night, ask your child to picture this activity, when and where she is doing it, and the feelings of satisfaction that she will get from it. Through this technique you may gradually make that image so powerful in her mind that she will in fact organize her daily schedule to include the activity that you both agree is valuable for her.

The fact that you value reading will be a great motivator for your child. Your example and your praise for reading cannot be overstated. But motivation is only the beginning. Habits of mind are built slowly over the years and result from repeated words and actions. You can foster the development of positive attitudes by following the four steps outlined in this chapter.

1. Help your child become aware that some people have positive attitudes about reading and writing.

2. Get your child to respond to and talk about an activity that represents the attitude.
3. Lead your child to say that she values reading books on certain subjects. She needs to say that she likes to do it.
4. Help your child make a place in her life for the kind of reading that she says she values. Then your child has a strong positive attitude that will serve her in all that she does.

Chapter Three

Improving your child's reading comprehension

'Tis but a base, ignoble mind that mounts
no higher than a bird can soar.
*— Shakespeare, **Henry V.***

The purpose for reading is to understand the printed message. All of our efforts, therefore, should be directed to that end—understanding. This is best achieved in a straightforward manner.

If your child demonstrates that he already understands the message, praise him and get out of the way. Don't dwell on specific comprehension activities when your child shows that the job is done. But since most children are regularly challenged by the textbooks and the stories they read, we parents often need to assist them by following a process that guides the mind as it struggles with ideas and events.

Think of the reading process as something one does before reading, during reading, and after reading. Almost any major activity requires preparation, engagement, and follow-up. When you go skiing, for instance, you select clothes, get appropriate boots and skis, and make sure everything is conditioned for the rigors of the ski slope. While skiing, you are conscious of direction, balance, maintaining control, and of course having a good time with your friends. Afterwards, you dry out your clothes, take a warm bath, and relive the events of the day to the amusement of your friends and relatives.

Before reading you get your mind ready for the message that you face. Especially if the material relates to school study, you want to discover what you *already* know about the subject. Can you bring to the front of your mind words or ideas associated with the topic? Are there some things that you would like to clarify, words that need explaining, a frame of reference that might make you more comfortable as you tackle the printed page? And what are your purposes for reading this book? Questions such as these go through the mind of the good reader as he prepares for a book. In helping your child, you should raise similar questions. By discussing them briefly, you can create a mindset that is confident and full of purpose.

> **How can I help my child understand what he reads?**

During reading you are pursuing a message, usually for a specific purpose—even if it is merely to outwit the detective in a murder mystery by predicting who the real culprit is. The effective reader constantly monitors his own understanding. In a sense, he keeps asking: "Am I learning anything yet?" or "Am I getting the information I need to achieve my purpose?" If the reader isn't learning or isn't achieving his purpose, then he needs to do something differently. We read to build meaning. If meaning is not being built or if purpose is not being met, then you want to change directions to make it meaningful. Do you need to reread at a slower pace? Did you miss an important item that is the key to your understanding? Do you have to look ahead to see if the upcoming events may clarify your understanding? Are the vocabulary and the concepts so difficult that you need to find an easier book, or to work on the vocabulary before proceeding? Perhaps you and the author are not in the same ballpark. The critical issue here is that your mind is always working, is always building meaning while reading. You can help your child by asking him what purpose he has set for reading and by telling him to keep in mind that his job is to make sense as he reads. When he feels that isn't happening, he should stop and discuss matters with you—or with his teacher. Then you can talk about looking ahead, or predicting, or working on difficult vocabulary and concepts.

After reading, an effective reader consolidates his understanding of the book or the text. Most simply he can do that with a summary. This can be either a written summary or one that is told to another person. Little children are often asked to retell a story they have read. This is a form of consolidation. It is a way for them to show that the main events are in place. Often times it is more effective to have children tell what the story means to them or to explain how they will use the ideas that they have worked on. In the case of a book, it may be quite appropriate to ask for a recommendation—"Who else should read this book? Do you want any of your friends or family to read it? Why?"

If we see reading as a thoughtful event, then we will prepare our minds before we focus our eyes intently on the printed page and follow up with a thoughtful consolidation of our understanding. The balance of this chapter will give you some specific activities that you can use to help your child before, during, and after reading.

Before reading

Vocabulary

Once your child has chosen a story for reading, look through it to find out if there are difficult or unfamiliar words. Depending on the situation, the two of you could either talk about the words before the child

How important are background and vocabulary?

reads the story or you could use the words in discussions afterwards. Chapter Four deals with the problems involved in addressing new words, and Chapter Five offers some suggestions on improving vocabulary. For now, let's look at ways in which you can help your child deal with new and difficult words within the context of a given story. The emphasis here will be on finding meaning rather than confronting specific technical problems such as word structure.

If it's obvious to you that a story your child plans to read will introduce some difficult words, it's a good idea to talk about those words beforehand. For example, if a second grader is about to read a book that mentions "cumulus clouds" or "alligators in the swamp," the child may have no idea of what *cumulus*, *alligator* or *swamp* refer to, and may not be able to link the words with the things they represent. Show pictures and use the words in simple sentences that define the words in context (such as "The white, fluffy cumulus clouds drifted across the clear sky."). This is especially important if the unfamiliar word is used in the story without any hints as to what it means. After the story you can reinforce the meaning of *cumulus* by asking your child to talk about cumulus clouds.

You may sometimes be able to highlight the meaning of words with pictures. For words that represent emotions or concepts, pictures may not be available. Ask your child to explain the words using them in short sentences. ("John was *proud* of himself for getting an A on the spelling test. He felt good because he knew he had worked hard and proved he could do it.") Whenever possible, use the context of the story to explain the meaning of words. As you know, many words shift their meaning as they are used in different contexts.

It's not always easy to tell whether a certain word is going to pose problems. If your child reads, "The dog can *run* fast," he may be confused when reading the sentence, "He will *run* for Congress this year," or "There was a *run* on the bank." (The Random House College Dictionary lists 135 definitions for the word *run*, including its many usages as a noun and a verb and even one listing as an adjective meaning "melted or liquefied.") Despite this multiple meaning problem, it's possible over time to understand various meanings by first figuring out how the word is used in a particular sentence or paragraph. If your child is reading something interesting but the story uses technical terms, he may "get through" the article, but much of what is read may not be very well understood. That's when you can help by discussing some of the technical terms and add to your child's understanding.

Purposes for reading

We read for different things and different reasons, and young readers need to set purposes so that they create some expectations. Of course you shouldn't impose your own purpose for reading on your child. You want him to think for himself. Therefore, discuss what he wants to get out of the story. In this way, your child learns to ask questions that the story may answer ("What problems might come up on a cross-country hike?" or "What would it feel like to practice hard for the big race and then lose?"). Keep in mind that there are different kinds of purposes. A story may be read to find out what happened when Jim and Ed went into a haunted house at night. After reading, you may want to challenge your child to decide if the actions of the characters were morally good. The two of you can discuss the purposes that were set, and you may learn why purposes were or were not met.

Before a child reads anything, he must have the background needed to understand it. After all, it would be difficult to understand a character's fear of the Everglades if you have no sense of that swampy environment and the animal life found there. That's the reason it helps to pick stories that interest your child. One purpose for reading could be to expose him to new information on personal interests. You can build on his interest in horse stories to expand his knowledge about the care and training of horses and about the difference between show horses, race horses, and pleasure horses. Another purpose for reading is to introduce your child to new areas of interest (knights and the Middle Ages, or life in primitive tribes in Australia, for instance), or to widen the child's understanding about a recent experience (for example, through a guidebook from a family trip). By fitting reading into daily life, you make it real and reduce the number of problems that might arise.

What are techniques to help my child monitor his own understanding?

At the end of this chapter you'll find a series of short stories designed for first-, second- and third- graders. They include questions about each story. The stories and questions can serve as models to show how you can first prepare your child for reading, and then follow up after reading.

During reading

Asking questions to aid thinking

Before your child reads a book or article, ask questions about the passage. This serves the two-fold purpose of focusing attention ("How many times did Bill try to make the team?") and setting a purpose for reading ("If a boy tried to get on the football team but didn't run fast enough, what could he do to have a better chance of making the team the next year?").

If your questions prove difficult, lead your child to appropriate answers by discussing what you would do to answer those questions. For example, you could ask what Bill did to make himself a better player and what the coach thought about the extra effort that Bill was making. Show how you would think through the problem. After all, this is not a test. You are both searching for solutions to your purpose questions. You could then reread the story with your child. In this way you help him to achieve success as a reader and, conversely, help to avoid the sense of failure that can dampen enthusiasm for reading.

After reading

Ordinarily you should not interrupt your child's reading. After he finishes, ask him to find the sentence that answers a question. This prompts rereading for a specific purpose. (For example, "Can you find the sentence in the story that tells when Frank decided he could land the airplane?") You can also ask questions that require interpretation of a passage. ("How did Johnny feel when his horse died?" "Why did the girls run away?") These kinds of questions allow your child to show his understanding in his own way.

If you believe it will help your child to focus better, you can ask questions that call for close attention to the content of the story: "Why did the people of the town want to cut down the old tree?" Questions can serve as a point of departure for a discussion of issues raised by a story: "Do you think the old tree in the park was as important as the new building that was built in its place?"

Hold a conversation

When a story is finished and the two of you talk about it, avoid giving the impression that your questions are part of a "test." Just hold a conversation. The child should be offered a chance to say what he thinks about the story. Here, there are no "right" answers, and your discussion may bring out interests or reading problems that can be addressed later. A question as simple as "Did you like the story?" or "Were there any parts you thought were a little hard to understand?" or "What parts were most interesting to you?" can open up wonderful opportunities for good talk about books.

The questions you ask should aid your child's thinking. "What do you think this word means?" "Why does a treasure hunt make such an interesting story?" "Were the characters wrong to do what they did?" "What did you like best about the story?" "Did you like reading about imaginary worlds?" Your underlying purpose as a parent is usually to spur your child to think. Help him become an active reader, one who is involved in the text.

One caution: don't overwhelm the child. Obviously, if you ask scores of questions about the same short reading passage, he is likely to become confused or feel that he is being tested. Think of a conversation with an adult about a book or a magazine article. Keep that frame of reference and your child will be eager to please you.

Sentence meaning

Very young children usually need regular help with reading. In their struggle to decipher the printed page, they may begin to concentrate on individual letters and words. Parents can help by reminding them that sentences are their major language units. You can draw your child's attention to the meanings of whole sentences by asking questions that require an understanding of groups of words. (For example, given the sentence, "Jimmy walked to the hardware store," you could ask, "To what kind of story did Jimmy go, and how did he get there?") Giving your child practice in completing sentences from a book is another way to remind him of the sentence unit. (For instance, you can ask what word best fits into the blank in the sentence: "When I'm tired at night, I get into bed and go to ____.")

Here are a few other ways you can help to increase

awareness of sentence meanings and story context.

➡ **Reading for sentence meaning.** If a single word is unfamiliar, it can interfere with the reader's ability to understand an entire sentence. When this happens, you should encourage your child to go back over the sentence and try to think of a word that makes sense in that spot. This helps him learn that discovering meaning, and not just pronouncing a word, is what matters most. As an example, in the passage, "She never had seen such a beautiful synagogue. She was happy to be celebrating a most important Jewish holy day there," a child may be able to figure out that the unfamiliar word *synagogue* is some kind of church. The context of two sentences brings a sense that "synagogue" is a place where Jewish people worship.

➡ **Allow the child to substitute words.** If a child understands the context of a story and picks up meaning along the way, he may be able to predict some appropriate words even if they are not the exact words in print. When this happens, you needn't correct the child. Your first concern is that he thinks and gets reasonable meaning from the text. For example, if the story says, "We saw a *herd* of cows on my uncle's farm," your child may read it as, "We saw a *bunch* of cows on my uncle's farm." He hasn't changed the meaning of the story and has shown that he is paying attention. If you stop your child and make him correct the word, he may give up a very useful, mature reading strategy of predicting meaning. First and foremost keep the focus on meaning—"Does that make sense?" You can always go back later and point out that there were many cows in the picture, and that is what "herd" means. At that point you can ask how that word begins ("h") and what sound—spelling pattern—he can use to recognize the word in the future (for example, herd sounds like *her* + *d*). You might also mention that the cows can be referred to as a *group* or *bunch,* but there are sometimes special words for groups of things, such as a *herd* of cows or a *flock* of birds. Ask if your child can think of any more words of this kind. You may be able to find a list of such "collective nouns" in a reference book.

Obviously, if a clearly incorrect word is substituted in a written sentence, you shouldn't ignore that. For instance, if the word *group* is read as *grow up,* it means he has substituted a word or phrase that does not make sense and he needs to rethink the situation and to refocus on meaning. Once again, you should avoid criticizing your child for being "wrong." In fact, you could point out that he made a good try at sounding out the word group. After the section is finished you can come back to the word and have your child use it in a sentence. You could even ask him to look for or draw pictures showing "groups" of things. For more help on dealing with unfamiliar words, see Chapter Four.

➡ **Supplying words in incomplete sentences.** A good way to get a child to think about the context of a sentence is to ask him to fill in a word that's missing from a sentence. In the sentence, "Mary saw a _____ flying in the sky," the child might suggest *bird, airplane, kite,* or *balloon* as the missing word. You could then be more specific by asking, "What can fly in the sky, and starts with the letter *B*?" Because there may be more than one possible answer (as here with *balloon* or *bird*), you may use pictures or additional clues: "What can fly and ends with the letter *D*?"

➡ **Matching sentences to pictures.** You can show your child a picture, offer several sentences that tell what the picture represents, and have him pick the sentence that best describes what is happening. Another way of approaching this is to give a sentence and have the child draw a picture to represent it. ("Two fish are swimming in a bowl.")

Stories for practice reading

On the next few pages are stories that you can use to practice some of the ideas in this chapter. The reading process involves getting the mind focused before reading; then reading with a purpose and monitoring your progress at making meaning; and, after reading, trying to wrap it up. If you work through some of these stories with your child, you will probably work most effectively by making these exercises a kind of conversation. We have given you a few ideas for those conversations before and after reading, but let the story topics and the natural drift of any conversation lead the two of you. As with any reading experience, you want your child to build meaning and to understand that he has to be an active and a thoughtful reader.

THE SCHOOL BUS DRIVER*
(Early First Grade)

Before reading

You can start by talking with your child about what a person might see on a bus ride: the people riding the bus, the things outside the window, and so on. You could lead into the story by saying it's about a bus driver who does funny things, and ask, "What do you suppose the bus driver does that's funny? Let's read the story and find out."

I go to school on a school bus.

My friends ride on the bus, too.

We like to ride on the school bus
because a funny woman drives the bus.

She drives and she sings.

She sings to the birds.

She sings to the cats.

She sings to my friends.

And we all sing, too.

* Ideas for this group of stories came from *Series r*, by Carl Smith and Ronald Wardhaugh. New York, N.Y.: Macmillan Pub. Co., 1975.

After reading
- Would you like to ride on that school bus?
- Why?
- Why do you think the children liked that bus driver?

Let your child express his or her own ideas but also join in the fun. Give your own ideas and just talk about the story as you might talk about a television show you had watched together.

THE SINGING FROG
(Late First Grade)

Before reading

This is a story about a most unusual frog. You might ask your child what a real frog would do, and then lead into this story about an imaginary frog who does things no one could ever guess.

Freddy Frog did not have many things.

He did not have a bike or a car.

He did have one old book that he read again and again.

And he had a little bed to sleep in, but that was all.

Freddy Frog did not have many things,
but he was happy by the lake.

He looked at the flowers, and he liked to dance.

But most of all Freddy Frog liked to sing.

In those days frogs did not sing.

They didn't think it was right for frogs to sing.

"Singing is for the birds," they said.

But Freddy Frog liked to sing.

And so he sang and sang because it made him happy.

Soon the other frogs tried to sing his song.

Can you sing Freddy Frog's song?

After reading

Perhaps the best way to finish this story is to have your child sing like a frog. Most children love to make up tunes with "ribbit ribbit" sounds. But you might also like to talk about what made this frog different from ordinary frogs.

THE BEAR WHO WANTED TO BE DIFFERENT
(Early Second Grade)

Before reading

This is about a bear who wanted to be different from all the other bears. What do you suppose a bear might do to try to be different? What might happen if a little bear tried to make himself look like some other animal? This story tells what happened when this bear tried to make himself look different.

A little black bear lived in the woods. He thought that he was very special. But he saw that one little black bear looked just the same as any other little black bear. That did not make him feel like a special bear. He wanted to be different.

One day he watched a deer eating leaves off the trees. He decided he wanted to be like the deer. He would try to look like the deer. He would eat leaves of the trees. Then he would be different from the other little bears. Then he would be very special.

So he found some branches and tied them tight on his head. Now he thought he looked like a deer. Then he tried to eat some leaves. They were not very tasty. They were not tasty like berries. He decided that maybe he would not eat leaves.

He went to show the other bears how special and different he was. But he did not look like a deer to them. They just asked him why he had branches on his head.

After reading
- Is this a sad story or a happy one?
- Why?

Everyone wants to be special, and you may want to talk about the special qualities that each of you possess. Being special doesn't mean that you have to look like someone else. Where did the little bear go wrong?

MARIA'S SURPRISE
(Second Grade)

Before reading

Begin by talking about things children have brought to school to show the other children. What could a child bring that would be really unusual and different from most things that are brought? This story is about a girl who brought a special surprise when it was her turn to share with the others in her class.

On Monday morning, Maria wore a pretty new dress when she walked into the class-room. Her eyes were very bright.

It was sharing time that morning, and Mrs. Green looked at Maria. "It's Maria's turn to share today," she said.

Maria walked to the door and opened it. She smiled and said, "You may come in now, Papa." Maria's father walked in with a big box of Mexican things from his store.

"This is my papa," said Maria. "His name is Mr. Martinez. He is going to show you some interesting things from Mexico."

All the boys and girls clapped, and Papa smiled a big smile.

After reading
- Do you think the title of the story is a good one?
- Why?

What other special surprises could children bring to class to share with their schoolmates? You might use this story to think about the kinds of things that Mr. Martinez might have showed the children in Maria's class. If you and your child have been to Mexico or to a Mexican store or restaurant, you can talk about that experience as an extension of this story.

LANA THE MUSICIAN
(Early Third Grade)

Before reading

You might talk with your child about his or her own experience with music, whether that involves singing or playing, listening to records, or seeing musicians on television. "What instrument do you think a little girl in the third grade might play?" This story will tell you.

Music filled Lana's house. Every afternoon mother played the piano. Each member of the family went off to different rooms of the house to practice their music.

Lana went to the laundry room to practice. Jasmine the cat went with her. Lana played a wooden recorder. The recorder had a mouthpiece for blowing and seven airholes. Also there was one airhole underneath which was meant just for her thumb. Lana was just beginning to learn how to play. She knew what to do to make the notes, but sometimes the notes didn't want to cooperate.

Jasmine hid in the laundry basket when Lana played. That made Lana laugh.

After reading

Most children will want to speculate why the cat hid in the laundry basket.

You could try to think of other instruments that third graders might play or discuss why each member of the family went to a different room of the house each afternoon. Practice, of course, is necessary for school work and sports, as well as music.

Would your child like to play a musical instrument? And practice regularly?

HERMAN THE TADPOLE
(Third Grade)

Before reading

This is a story about an unusual tadpole. What do you suppose real tadpoles do all day? What could one tadpole do that would make him the leader of all the other tadpoles?

Herman lived in a pond which was clean and cool. Everything seemed peaceful and quiet. Herman and his friends loved to play games and to dart here and there in the pond.

Now, he did have some problems. You see, he was very small, like all tadpoles. Snakes, fish, and even frogs were always trying to catch him for dinner. But they never caught Herman. He was fast and clever, and he always knew where to hide.

Since Herman was the fastest and the smartest of all the tadpoles, he became the leader.

He led his friends up and down the pond in search of food. And they always found some.

The other tadpoles thought Herman was the smartest tadpole they knew.

After reading.

You could easily turn this into a discussion of pond life, but first your child needs to understand that tadpoles are baby frogs. As tadpoles, however, they just don't look like frogs. And it should be interesting to your child to learn that one of the dangers tadpoles face is from frogs.

Where could you get more information on pond life? The library, certainly; and also the encyclopedia. Children's magazines often have features on animal life.

Just as a story, it is fun to speculate on why the other tadpoles would follow Herman as their leader. Where do leaders show up among children in school?

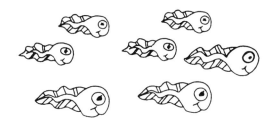

Chapter Four

Skills for identifying words

A page digested is better than a volume hurriedly read.
—Thomas Macaulay

When your child is stumped by a new or difficult word, you can help him work through the problem and learn from it. A few word identification strategies will give your child confidence in figuring out new words in the future. This chapter deals with some of the skills and strategies a young learner needs for dealing with such words.

A strategy for recognizing words

Use cues

Before looking at specific word skills, learn to follow this strategy for tackling unfamiliar words. Below are five steps a learner can follow in dealing with unfamiliar words. But if your child figures out the word after step 1 or step 2, that's as far as he needs to go. When reading, we want to get the message (or the unknown word) as quickly and directly as we can. We therefore use as few cues as possible to decipher the print and keep the message flowing. That's the goal of

What can I do to help my child figure out unfamiliar words?

all word identification strategies—keep the printed message flowing. You can use these steps as you help your child figure out unknown words. Gradually he will learn how to address these problems on his own because this five-step strategy will become automatic. Ask your child these questions in succession:

1. Do the words around the problem word give you a hint of what that new word is or what it means? (Context clues)

2. Does the beginning sound of the problem word, along with the rest of the sentence, help you figure out what that new word is? (Context plus initial sound)

3. Do the first two steps, along with looking at the final sound of the word, help you discover what the word is? (Context, initial and final sound)

4. Does the word have sound-spelling patterns that you recognize? Or does it have recognizable parts, as in *barnyard* or *rereading* (re/read/ing)? (Context plus patterns)

5. If you still can't solve the problem word, ask someone about it or use the dictionary to figure out how the word is pronounced and what it means. (Seek help)

At first you'll have to remind your child to go through these steps, but over time they'll become more automatic. Remember, use as few steps, as few cues as are needed to get the word and then keep moving. Here's an example of the process:

The brown fox *jumped* over the lazy dog.

- Context: The fox *does something* over the dog.
- Initial sound: *j* as in *June.*
- Final sound: *ed* as in *camped.*
- Sound-spelling pattern: c-v-cc gives the *u* a short sound as in *cup.* Add this to what you know about the beginning and ending sounds of the word.
- Ask someone what the word is, or look up its pronunciation in the dictionary.

The idea here is to identify the word in the fewest possible steps; the child continues reading as soon as the word registers in his mind.

Using the eyes and ears in identifying words

Children know a lot about the print world before they start school. Books, newspapers, signs, television ads, and room decorations give children a sense that printed messages are important and are a normal part of today's world. What you can do as a parent is help your child solve the mysteries of our alphabetic spelling system. In English we represent words and word sounds through patterns of letters and open spaces, that is, when we write we set off words with spaces. In our casual conversation, however, it is not easy to distinguish individual words. Think about two people entering the kitchen and saying these things:

First person: "Ja-eet?"
Second person: "Na. Jew?"

Translation:

First person: "Did you eat?"
Second person: "No. Did you?"

You can begin to appreciate one of the problems

that young learners have in trying to translate that kind of collapsed speech into a print environment where each word is set off with open spaces, and particular sounds are represented by particular letters. Part of learning to read, therefore, is paying attention to word sounds. You probably started that process when your child was in the crib. You held a round object over your child and said, "Ball. Ball. See the pretty ball." Or you took your child's hand and placed it on your nose: "Nose. Nose. Daddy's nose."

You gave your child a lesson in language and also began helping her learn that different objects are distinguished by different sounds. And as you touched her ears, and fingers, and toes, she heard some words that sounded quite different—*eyes, hands,*—and words that sounded alike: *nose, toes.* Over time, she learned even the fine distinction between the sounds of *nose* and *toes,* and she could point to the right body part (eyes, ears, nose, toes) when you asked in full sentence: "Where's Marla's nose?" "Where are Marla's toes?" So your child developed a sophisti-

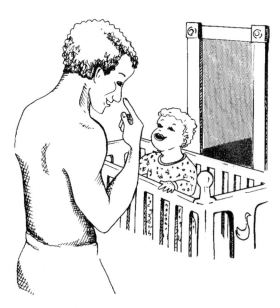

cated sense of word sounds and language sounds in the first two or three years of his or her life.

By age five or six, when most children begin formal reading instruction in school, your child has become quite adept at listening to a stream of language sounds and knowing what it all means: "Pick up ya toys, puteminabox, n hopinatub." Learning to read printed statements is partly a process of keeping the context of the message in mind, partly a process of picking up enough graphic cues to trigger a speech-like flow of language. Most people call those graphic cues *phonics*, that is, the sound-letter correspondence that helps readers associate the printed words with the sounds they hear in speech.

Are there phonics exercises I can use to help my child relate speech and printed language?

There is no magic set of phonics rules that will automatically make reading easy for your child. But this chapter gives you a number of guidelines and practice activities that you can use to help your child realize that there are borderlines to print. English spelling makes sense, and she can gradually master those sound-letter patterns to use in figuring out words on the printed page.

If your child reads smoothly and comprehends well, don't insist on doing the phonics exercises in this chapter. He's already doing what's important—reading fluently and understanding the message. If, on the other hand, he stumbles, asks for help, or doesn't understand certain sound-spelling patterns, then use the activities here to guide his understanding and to give him practice. These activities start with what every English speaker already knows—the sounds of words.

Word Differences

Objective

To have your child hear differences in a series of spoken words.

Procedure

Say two words and ask the child if they are the same or different. Start with simple one-syllable words that are obviously different (such as *car–dog*), to make a clear contrast. Then move to pairs of words that are alike (such as *big–pig*; *fat–cat*; *pin–pen*). If your child has no trouble with these pairs, use more than two words at a time, or longer words, for example, different forms of the same word (as in *runner––running* or *act–acted*).

Variation

Ask your child to think of other words like *runner–running* and to list as many as he can.

kick	kicker	kicking
act	actor	acting
play	player	playing
cook	_____	_____
sew	_____	_____
writer	_____	_____

Turn this into a game or a contest that you can turn to now and then. It helps your child realize that words are interesting and are marked by rather small distinguishing features. These exercises turn up your child's antennae.

L I S T E N I N G   E X E R C I S E

Hearing Small Differences in Words

Objective

To have your child figure out exactly what makes two or more words different from each other.

Procedure

Say two words that are different, but have similarities, such as the same first consonant (*cap–can* or *fit–fin*). Another way of doing this is to say words that rhyme (*say–pay*). Ask your child how the words are different in their sounds (the beginning *s* and *p* sounds) and how they are alike (they both end with an *ay* sound). Here are other samples:

rat–cat
rag–ran
man–men
beat–boat

Variation

Say a word and have your child repeat it. Then say two other words, and ask which of the words rhyme with the first one. Example: "Which words rhyme with *cat? Cow–hat–car–big–fat.*" Say the words slowly, so the child can answer after each one. "The next word is *run.* Which of these words rhymes with *run? Rain–rub–sun–bun.*

Follow-up

As a game, see how many rhyming pairs your child can make: rain/pain, stem/gem, rot/pot, and so on. Young children love rhyming activities and will often fill in a rhyming word at the end of a jingle. Mother Goose nursery rhymes provide you with excellent sources; so do simple children's songs.

Using Context and Initial Consonant

Objective

To use the first consonant sound in a word as a clue to what the word is.

Procedure

Say a short sentence in which one word is missing. Example: *The duck was swimming in the l___.* Tell your child that the first sound of the missing word is "l". What word starting with the *l*-sound would tell us where the duck was swimming? (lake) Use the same sentence, but with a different missing word (such as *The duck was swimming in the w___* (water), or *The duck was swimming in the p___.* (pool or pond)

Variation

You want your child to use the context of a sentence to figure out unknown words. Show him sentences in a newspaper where you have blocked off one word. Give him the initial consonant and ask him to complete the sentence as best he can. At first use sentences with simple words:

The man was walking his d____.
The b____was flying above us.

The first step is to help you child realize that the sentence gives him clues to unknown words, and the beginning of the word helps, too.

70

L I S T E N I N G   E X E R C I S E

What's that Word?

Objective
To pick out unclear words or phrases while listening to continuous text.

Procedure
Children need to make sense from what they hear as well as from what they read. Select a story that fits your child's age and read to her. Ask her to stop you when she doesn't understand a word or phrase. It doesn't matter whether the problem lies with your enunciation or with your child's not knowing the meaning of a word. She asks, "What's that word?" anytime she wants clarification. The exercise helps your child distinguish meaningful from non-meaningful words.

Your response should be to reread the sentence and to ask what makes sense in the troublesome spot. Then pronounce the word clearly and explain its meaning. Ask your child to repeat the word and then move on. Here is an example of a text that should raise questions:

Three gerbils escaped from their cage and ran into a meadow. They were so happy to be free that they were not careful. Suddenly a *zoton* swooped down and snatched up the last gerbil in line. The other two scurried down a *curleycue* hoping to find safety. Before they could plan to recapture the third gerbil, they heard the slithering movement of a *leeringulp* coming towards them. Up the curleycue they zipped and ran to a hollow log to plot the escape of their friend.

("Zoton" is an imaginary bird who acts like a hawk. "Curleycue" is an imaginary hole in the ground made by the "leeringulp," an imaginary lizard-like creature, who loves to gulp down rodents.)

Variation

Read from a book or a newspaper and ask your child to stop you when a word doesn't make sense. Remind him that you want him to make sense of the passage and this is one way that the two of you can pay attention to the sound and meaning of words, even nonsense words.

Follow-up

You might also challenge your child to read a passage to you and have you also ask: "What's that word?"

V I S U A L   E X E R C I S E

Match Letters of the Alphabet

Objective

To find out if your preschool child can recognize and match individual letters of the alphabet.

Procedure

Print letters on a card. You can use all capitals, all lower case, or a mixture, depending on your child's own abilities and needs. Put several of the letters in a row, making sure one or more of the letters are the same as the one you're going to ask the child to match. Say a letter (or show it written on another card) and have the child point to and say that letter when he finds it in the row. Example: Place the letters D G R B E G in front of the child, then say or show the letter G, and have him say it and point to it each time it appears in the row.

Variation

Starting the same way as above, have your child place the matching letter on the one you said or showed him.

Follow-up

If your child is having trouble with certain letters, you can practice those separately or compare them to other letters until the child becomes familiar with the troublesome letter.

V I S U A L E X E R C I S E

Match Short Words

Objective

To have the child identify words that are repeated in a series.

Procedure

Write several short words on cards (one word per card). Make sure one of the words appears more than once. Ask your child to find the word that is repeated. Example: set cards with the words FOG HOT HAT RAT HOT in front of the child, and have him find the repeated word.

Variation:

Place cards, each with a different word on it, in front of the child. Say or show your child one of the words and have him match it with one of the words on the cards. Example: put cards with the words CAR GOOD UP EAR BOY in front of the child, show him another card with the word EAR on it (or say it), and have him find the card with the matching word.

Follow-up:

As with letters in the previous exercise, you can help your child practice entire words that prove difficult.

Match Rhyming Words

Objective

To have your child match rhyming words.

Procedure

Write several words on cards and lay them out so your child can read them. Two or more of the words should rhyme, but don't repeat any words. Tell your child to find the words that rhyme. Example: given the words CAR HOT BOY FAR GOOD, the child should point to and say the rhyming words CAR and FAR.

Variation

Place cards, each with a different word on it, before the child. Say a word or show a card with a word on it, and have the child find a word that rhymes. Example: lay out cards with the words BOOT TOE NOSE RUN EAR, and say or show the word FUN. Have your child find the rhyming word RUN. You could also point to a word and ask the child to say it and give you a word that rhymes with it. It's best to start with words in which the ending sound is spelled the same way.

Follow-up

Sing a song or recite a jingle with rhyming words. Ask your child to pick out the words that rhyme. Then write them on a card or a piece of paper for your child to see.

V   I   S   U   A   L   E   X   E   R   C   I   S   E

Identifying Consonant Sounds

Objective

To have your child match up words with the same beginning or ending consonant.

Procedure

Write 6–12 words on individual cards. Have your child find a pair with the same first or last consonant. After she has matched the words, ask her to pronounce the words to hear the similarity in the way they begin or end. Here are some sample words:

fill	hot	run	said
let	soon	red	far
deer	foot	big	did

Some words will fit in both categories: *run* begins with the same letter as *red*, and *red* also ends with the same letter as *did* and *said*. Have your child find words with the same first consonant (*fill–far–foot, soon–said, deer–did, run–red,* and words with the same ending consonant (*run–soon, far–deer, big–leg, hot–foot, red–did–said*).

Variation

Use words with more complex beginning sounds (*bl-, blue, blush, blast; dr-, dress, drink, drive; ch-, chick, church, change,* and so on). You might also give your child a list of words that are all different, and have him come up with words with the same beginning or ending sounds as those on the list.

Follow-up

If a difficulty appears, you can use similar drills concentrating on the troublesome letters.

Using phonics to identify words

The "code"

Our alphabet is a set of visual symbols that stand for speech sounds. Early in the process of learning to read, a child must learn how to handle this *code*, that is, how to translate the symbols into sounds and vice versa. As your child matures and becomes more skilled in handling written language, the translating becomes more and more automatic. However, before this can happen, a child must master the connection between language that is heard and language that is seen.

Although the link between spoken and written English is not always consistent, a child must still deal with the sound-symbol relationship of the alphabet as a step toward learning to read. In our written language there are many rules, but we can still make some general statements that can be helpful to a young reader.

The most important point to make about the alphabet is that it's divided into consonants and vowels. The vowels are *a, e, i, o u*, and sometimes *y* and *w*. Vowels are the most important sound elements of the language, because they carry the open, unblocked sounds of the words, and can be pronounced easily when separated from words. Consonants interrupt and modify vowel sounds, turning those sounds into recognizable words (for example adding the *d* sound at the beginning of the *ay* vowel sound gives us the word *day*, and putting a *t* after the vowel sound *ea* creates the word *eat*.

Vowel sounds can be long or short. They are long when pronounced as they appear in the alphabet: *a* as in *able*, *e* as in *equal*, *i* as in *ice*, *o* as in *over*, and *u* as in *use*. These same letters can also represent short vowel sounds: *a* (*act*), *e* (*egg*), *i* (*if*), *o* (*nod*), and *u* (*up*).

Sometimes, certain combinations of letters make the vowel sound different from either the short or long sounds: the *a* in *car* is modified by the *r* that follows it, and the *o* and *i* in *boil* also take on different sounds than usual when put together.

What are some of the patterns to written English?

The idea behind what is called phonics is to teach reading students that they can group vowels and consonants into usable patterns. Encourage your child to use these patterns. He can search the daily newspaper for words that fit the rule or rules he has just learned. Of course, a beginner may be able to pick out the rules only in one-syllable words.

The five most important phonics rules appear below. They should be of help to you as you guide your child through early reading efforts.

➡ **Short vowel rule.** If there is only one vowel in a word or syllable, the vowel is usually a short sound if it appears at the beginning or in the middle of the word. Some examples are *at, fed, bit, cot,* and *up.*

➡ **Long vowel rule 1.** If a two-vowel word or syllable has a silent *e* at the end, the first vowel in the word usually has a long sound, as in words such as *make, scene, time, tone,* and *tune.*

➡ **Long vowel rule 2.** If there is a double vowel in a word or syllable, the first vowel usually has a long sound and the second vowel is silent. We can see this in words including *rain, lean,* and *roam.*

➡ **Murmur rule.** If a vowel is followed by an *r,* the sound of the vowel is neither long nor short; it takes on a different sound: *car, perk, fir, or,* and *hurt.*

➡ **Diphthong rule.** In some words with double vowels, the sounds of the two letters are linked together; for instance, *ou* in *house, ow* in *now, oi* in *oil,* and *oy* in boy.

Phonics exercises

Phonics guidelines teach children to de-code written words into the sounds they represent. Here are some exercises you can use to help your child.

How can my child use these patterns to improve his reading independence?

➥ **Connecting the sound and the letter.** Make the sound of the letter that you are teaching your child, and have him imitate what you do. Show how the mouth is shaped and how the lips and tongue move when you form the letter. For example, you might contrast the part the tongue plays in making the *d* sound with the role of the lips in forming the sound of the letter *p*, as in *dog* and *pet*: I have a pet dog.

➥ **Show the link between the sound of a word and its written form.** It is best to use short words when explaining sound-letter connections. Since these phonics sounds appear only in whole words, always demonstrate sound-letter connections in real words. For example, the sound of the letters *b*, *u*, and *g* will make more sense to the child if combined into the word *bug*.

➥ **Changing letters to show changes in sounds.** Use a series of words like the following to show how small changes in sound make a new word.

bit—bat

bat—cat

cat—cab

cab—car

car—far

As you can see, after each change the last word in

the pair becomes the first word in the next pair. The child learns that different letters represent different sounds, and different sounds change meanings.

➡ **Words that rhyme.** As a child tries to find rhyming words, he becomes aware of words that have the same middle and ending sounds. Give your child a word and ask him for words that rhyme with it. You can approach this as a variation of the previous drill and ask the child to make rhymes by substituting the first letter in a word with other letters:

ran — can — man

fin — pin — win

cop — hop — shop

➡ **Word beginnings and endings.** Sometimes your child will be able to figure out a word by looking at the first and last letters and thinking about what sounds they represent. Context clues can help, too. For example, if the child sees the word *sofa*, he might not recognize it, but he can sound out the *s* and *o* and figure it out from the rest of the sentence: The boy sat down on the big *sofa*.

The general theme of phonics (decoding) is that English spelling is consistent enough to help readers with most words. By learning rules about sound-symbol relationships and word order, a child gradually learns to make predictions about new words. By the time they get into the first grade, most children have a surprising number of these rules about word order and context in their minds. With phonics, we try to build on this basic knowledge and help them recognize some of the spelling patterns used in English. This reassures children and gives them confidence that they will gradually master the sound-spelling system. Remember that the goal here is to enable your child to use phonics in reading, not recite rules from memory.

The exercises that follow give your child a chance to apply phonics rules.

Consonant and Vowel Identification—by Name

Objective

To have your child identify letters by name and tell whether the letters are consonants or vowels.

Procedure:

Write a series of letters in no special order, and in both capitals and lower case. You could also use letters written on cards for earlier exercises; just place several of them in a row. Ask your child to name each letter and to say whether it's a vowel or a consonant.

Examples:

B G r H t u E j

o f T S v a l n

Q z p X y W i M

Variation

Show the child the series of letters and say one of them. Have him point to the letter you say, and tell you if it's a consonant or a vowel. Keep picking letters at random from the series.

P H O N I C S   E X E R C I S E

Consonant and Vowel Identification — by Sound

Objective

To have your child identify the first sound in words, tell whether it's a vowel or consonant, and think of another word beginning with the same sound.

Procedure

Write a series of words, or use those made for earlier exercises. Each word should begin with a single consonant (*cat, dog, top, fun,* etc.). Say each word and have your child tell you:

(1) what letter stands for the first sound in the word;

(2) whether that letter is a vowel or a consonant; and

(3) another word that starts with the same sound.

Variation

Show your child a group of words. Say one of them; have him find it and tell you whether the first sound is a vowel or a consonant. Ask for another word that starts with the same sound.

Recognizing the Beginning Consonant

Objective

To have your child identify the first consonant in a nonsense word and give another word that starts with the same consonant. This is similar to the previous exercise, but nonsense words are used so that the attention is on the sounds and letters heard at the beginning of the words.

Procedure

Say a group of nonsense words, each starting with a clear, single consonant. After each one, have your child tell you the beginning letter and another word that starts with the same consonant. Some nonsense words that might be used are:

BARG	COBE	DOP	FURB	GUG
HAB	JID	KAG	LORP	MEP
NOP	POLD	ROG	SARD	TEB

You may want to start with one example to show your child how it words: "If I say BARG, you could tell me it starts with the letter ___. That's right, _b_. Now tell me another word that starts with the same sound as BARG." (BOY, BIRD, etc.)

Variation

Show the child each nonsense word, have him pronounce it or at least identify the first consonant and give another word starting the same way.

P H O N I C S   E X E R C I S E

First Consonant Clapping Game

Objective

To practice listening for the first consonant in words.

Procedure

Make a separate card for each consonant to be practiced. List words that start with the letter on each card. Among the words should be some that your child can't spell, so all of his attention is on the first consonant. Using a dictionary, you can come up with a list of words of varying difficulty. For example, the *b* card might include *babble, baboon, bachelor, bacteria, badger* and *balance*. On the *m* card you could write *macaroon, mace, mackerel, madrigal,* and so on. To help your child practice the first consonant *b*, you would say some of the words from that card mixed with words from other cards. Each time your child hears a word beginning with the letter *b* he should clap; if the word doesn't start with a *b*, he shouldn't clap.

Variation

You can take the same approach in practicing consonants at the end of words. Clap when you hear the *t* sound at the end of words.

P H O N I C S   E X E R C I S E

Final Consonant Riddle Game

Objective

To practice listening for the final consonants, and making the connection between the sounds and letters for those consonants.

Procedure

Print riddles on cards, and give a clue about the answer word and its final consonant. Here are some examples:

*I am thinking of a word that ends like **red**. It is a place to sleep. What is it?* (bed)

*I am thinking of a word that ends like **man**. It is a time when we eat lunch. What is it?* (noon)

*I am thinking of a word that ends like **miss**. Dad uses a mower on it. What is it?* (grass)

You can read each riddle to your child, and tell him to give you the answer word and its final consonant. You may also want him to write the answer, or pick it from a group of words you've written on cards.

Variation

You can follow similar steps in working with your child on first consonants.

P H O N I C S   E X E R C I S E

Consonant Digraph "Grab Game"

Objective

To practice the sound-symbol link in consonant digraphs (two-letter combinations which have a different sound than the two letters alone would have: *ch, sh, ng,* etc.).

Procedure

Print consonant digraphs on small cards. Some digraphs come up most often at the beginnings of words (*wh, qu*), others are usually found at the ends of words (*ck, ng*), and there are those that may appear at either end (*ch, sh*). Here are some sample cards:

Make a list of words beginning with consonant digraphs (*choose, when, shut, quick, then, chop, shore, that,* and so on). Place the digraph cards in front of your child and say a word from the list. The child should point to the correct card and tell you what the digraph is. Follow the same procedure for words that end with digraphs. If you think your child can handle it, you could work with digraphs in the middle of words, too, as in re*qu*est, a*ch*ieve, no*th*ing, a*wh*ile, etc.

Consonant Blends

Objective

To have your child identify the sound of consonant blends, and to think of words that contain the blends. Consonant blends are pairs of consonants that are pronounced with no break between them (*bl* as in *blue*, *cr* in *creek*, *dr* in *drill*, and so on).

Procedure

Write several consonant blends on cards and show them to your child one at a time. Tell him to say the sound the letter pair makes, and ask for a word that has the blend in it. It's easiest to come up with words with the blends at the beginning.

BLEND	POSSIBLE WORDS
tr	train, tree, truck
dr	draw, dream, drag
bl	blue, blow, blend
gl	glow, glue, glad
br	brown, breeze, brag
sl	sleep, slow, slip
fr	fry, free, from
gr	green, grass, grow
cl	close, clean, clip
cr	crow, cream, creek
fl	flow, fly, fling
st	stop, story, sting
pl	play, plow, please

P H O N I C S E X E R C I S E

Consonant Blends

Objective

To have your child think of words that begin with certain consonant blends.

Procedure

Say pairs of letters that form consonant blends. Ask your child to write those consonants and say the sound they make when combined. Then the child should say or write a word with the blend in it. For example, if you gave your child the letters *g-r*, he would write those letters and say or write a word such as *green, grow,* or *grass.*

Some blends that can be used include:

B — L

T — R

G — L

S — T

D —R

P — L

F — L

P H O N I C S   E X E R C I S E

Long Vowels

Objective

To practice recognizing the letter symbol for each long vowel, and to come up with words that have the same vowel sound.

Procedure

Write short words on cards. Each word should contain a long vowel sound. These long sounds usually appear at the beginning or in the middle of words, as in *a*ble, t*a*pe, *e*qual, r*e*cede, *i*ce, p*i*pe, *o*ver, h*o*pe, *u*se, and r*u*de. Show each card to your child, or say the word and have him name the vowel and another word with the same vowel sound. You could make this more challenging by giving a word with the vowel at the beginning and asking for a word with that sound in the middle (or vice versa). This step will obviously be easier for an older child.

P H O N I C S   E X E R C I S E

Short Vowels

Objective
To practice recognizing the letter that stands for each short vowel and thinking of other words that have the same sound in them.

Procedure
Follow the same directions as in the previous exercise, but use words with short vowel sounds at the beginning or in the middle (at, flat, edge, west, it, sniff, office, hot, up, tuck). Try to avoid having the child just give you a rhyming word each time (fat-cat, hot-pot, etc.). If need be, you can ask for something other than a word that rhymes, or you could use words with more than one syllable (attack, effort, snicker, opportunity, pumpkin), which are more difficult to rhyme.

P H O N I C S E X E R C I S E

Long and Short Vowels

Objective

To practice telling long and short vowel sounds apart in pairs of words.

Procedure

Write pairs of words on cards, but make sure the words in each pair use the same vowel. One word should have a short vowel sound and the other, a long sound (rat-rate, for example). Show or say the words to your child, and ask him which one has the long vowel sound. The long vowel sound may be more obvious in words with a silent e at the end (cap-cape, bit-bite), so use some pairs that don't follow that pattern. Here are some other example pairs you could use:

hut-cute	pat-tape	pop-boat
rope-top	even-ever	met-meat
hit-nice	up-usual	mad-maid

As we've done here, you should mix up the order so the word with the long vowel sound doesn't always appear in the same position. Some of the words you use might contain several vowels, so you may want to underline the vowel that you plan to emphasize.

P H O N I C S   E X E R C I S E

Vowels Controlled by the Letter R

Objective

To practice using vowels which are changed from their usual long or short sounds by a following letter *r* (these are known as *r-controlled vowels*).

Procedure

Use the following list to practice identifying the vowel + r combination in each word. Have the child read from the list and give you the *r*-controlled vowel. After a number of examples, ask the child to state what she thinks happens when a vowel is followed by an *r*. (It is modified.)

ar	ar	er	or
farm	care	her	for
star	scare	under	horn
car	beware	term	corn
barn	bare	herd	horse
hard	flare	perch	form

or	ir	ur
word	bird	burn
work	girl	fur
worm	dirt	turn
worry	fir	curl
worst	stir	hurl

P H O N I C S   E X E R C I S E

Diphthongs

Objective

To practice recognizing and using diphthongs (gliding speech sounds formed by connecting two vowels such as the *oi* in *coin* and *ou* in *out*).

Procedure

Using the following list, have your child identify the two vowels involved in each diphthong. Mix words from different lists so you don't emphasize one diphthong more than others. You can also use these words in some of the earlier exercises.

oi	oy	ou	ow
coin	boy	trousers	flowers
soil	toy	outside	showers
boil	joy	mountain	howl
oil	oyster	house	down
join	Roy	loud	how
point	loyal	around	crown
noise	enjoy	mouse	brown
spoil	destroy	couch	growl
choice	voyage	ground	coward
moisture	decoy	blouse	prowl

Decoding by looking at word structure

Breaking words into their parts to find meaning

What a word means and how it is pronounced may change if prefixes and suffixes are added (as in *pre*fix or add*ed*), if compounds are created (such as warehouse), if the word has an inflectional ending (for example, the s in hide*s*), and so on. We can dis-connect the parts of words, to re-view how they are com-pose-d. Adults know how to do this from experience, and from what they learned in early reading instruction. Your child can gain more control by becoming familiar with prefixes and suffixes.

> *How can breaking word down into its parts help a child learn the word?*

Over time, your child must learn to break words down into meaningful parts, and to recognize and understand these parts. It's not always easy, but there are many structure hints that can be of help. Some of them follow.

➥ **Root word.** This is the base of a word, not modified by a prefix, suffix, or inflectional ending. The root remains the same even when a prefix or suffix is attached (for instance, *bound: bound*ed, re*bound*, *bound*less).

➥ **Compound word.** A compound word is made up of two or more root words combined into a single word. Sometimes, the compound combines the meanings of the original two words, (as in *classroom*), but in other cases, a whole new meaning results (as in the word *broadcast*).

➥ **Prefix.** A prefix changes the meaning of the root word by attaching something to the beginning of the word. For example, *un* attached to the word *worthy* gives it an opposite meaning, while the *re* attached to *wrap* means the action is repeated.

➡ **Suffix.** It's possible to change the meaning of the root by attaching something at the end of the word. The ending *less* put after the word *worth* gives it a different meaning, as does *ful* when placed after *wonder*.

➡ **Contraction.** This is a shortened form of two words combined into one. In this process, some letters are dropped from the word that is created, and the missing letters are replaced with an apostrophe ('). In this way, *he is* becomes *he's*, *can not* turns into *can't*, and *she will* is changed to *she'll*. Sometimes, there may be more than one way to make a contraction: *He is not* can be rewritten as *he's not* or *he isn't*.

Helping your child understand word structure

You can start helping your child recognize the structure of words as soon as he begins to read. At first, it's enough to just point out some of these elements, especially in simple cases. You can show, for example, that a word such as *boy* is made plural just by adding the letter *s*, or that compound words are formed by putting two words together: *football, sunshine.* More complicated examples can wait until your child has mastered basic skills.

How can I show how prefixes, suffixes, and contractions change the word's meaning?

There is one logical sequence you can follow as you work with your child. The exercises at the end of this section will be introduced in this same order. You can change the sequence according to the needs of your child or to mirror the order of the books that he's using in school.

- Basic words (*cat, tree, run, the* and so on)
- Inflectional endings (*-s, -es, -ed, -ing*)
- Compound words (*sailboat, baseball*)
- Prefixes (*mis*match, *un*tie)
- Suffixes (care*ful*, care*less*)
- Contractions (*they're, isn't*)

For the most part, simple examples of inflectional endings, compound words and contractions, similar to those below, are discussed during the first grade. More complex word changes are presented in second and third grade.

- Inflectional endings:
  Simple plurals formed by adding *s* (animals, birds, books).

  The present and past tense and the present participle (the -*ing* form) of basic verbs (*ask, asks, asked, asking; jump, jumps, jumped, jumping*).

  A limited number of possessive forms (*'s*) that may appear in stories (the *bird's* nest, the *boy's* book, *John's* coat, *Mary's* hat).

- Compound words:
  Children gradually compound words; these will be made up of pairs of words that are themselves familiar (*everyone, everywhere, afternoon, anything, breakfast, without*).

- Contractions:
  Some of the most common contractions may be taught to first graders (such as *can't, don't, I'm, I'll, isn't, that's*).

Word structure exercises

On the following pages you'll find exercises designed to highlight skills that your child will need as he deals with word structure. If you find that the child would benefit from more practice on a particular skill, simply return to the exercises on that point.

W O R D   S T R U C T U R E   E X E R C I S E

Plural Endings -s, -es

Objective

To practice forming plurals by adding -s, and to start working with words that require -es for the plural.

Procedure

Print nouns on individual cards, each appearing in singular form on one card and in plural form on another. At first, use words whose plural only requires an -s. Later, you can work with words requiring -es (*churches, lunches, foxes, kisses, watches,* etc.). Show each card to your child and ask if it is singular or plural. If the word is in plural form, you can also ask for its singular form, and vice versa.

Variation

It's also a good idea to have your child use both forms of the noun in a sentence. When the noun is used as a direct object, this will be fairly simple (*I see the boy* and *I see the boys*), but when the noun is used as a subject, and changes from singular to plural, the verb changes too (*The car is red, The cars are red*).

W O R D   S T R U C T U R E   E X E R C I S E

Plural Endings -s, -es, -ies

Objective

To practice making plurals, using not only *-s* and *-es*, but also *-ies* for words ending in *y* (*city, cities*, for example).

Procedure

Make a set of cards with a singular noun on each card. Make another set just with the plural endings *-s*, *-es*, and *-ies*. Be sure to have enough plural cards to match all the words in each grouping. Here are some words that you can use:

-s	**-es**	**-ies**
boy	dress	fly
bird	lunch	puppy
school	fox	city
book	glass	bunny
girl	kiss	pony
hat	box	party
pet	ranch	lady
door	watch	candy
window	dish	baby

Your child should pick one of the noun cards and try to figure out which ending card goes with it to make the word plural, as shown below.

Variation

As a game for two or more children, shuffle all of the cards together. Deal out five cards to each player and put the rest in the middle of the playing area. The first player draws the top card from the deck and tries to match it with a card in his hand to form a plural word. If he can make a match, he can lay down the two cards in front of him. That player then lays down a card, placing it next to the deck. The next player can either pick up that card or draw the next one from the deck. Whoever is first to use up all of his cards wins.

W O R D   S T R U C T U R E   E X E R C I S E

Choosing a Plural Ending

Objective

To practice choosing the correct plural form for various singular nouns.

Procedure

Write a list of singular nouns and follow each one with three possible spellings for its plural form. For beginners, you could limit your list to nouns whose plural is formed simply by adding an *-s* or an *-es*. For older children you can make the list as challenging as you wish. Here is a list that includes many variations of plurals.

Singular	Pick the correct plural form		
ship	shipes	ships	shipers
leaf	leafs	leafes	leaves
cow	cows	cowes	cowers
woman	womans	womanes	women
fox	foxes	foxs	fox
doll	dolles	dols	dolls
army	armys	armies	armyes
man	men	mans	menes

If you're working with an older child, you may want to focus on those nouns whose plural forms require a greater change to the root word than simply adding an ending (for example, *mouse-mice; foot-feet*).

WORD STRUCTURE EXERCISE

Verb Endings

Objective

To have your child pick the correct verb form from among three choices given in a sentence.

Procedure

Write complete sentences, but include three possible forms for the verb. Have your child read the sentence, and pick the correct verb form. If you like, you can link sentences together to form a *story*. By taking that approach, the learner has to pick the right verb form, or the story won't make sense. Here's a sample story:

Yesterday, John (lose, lost, loses) *his hat on the playground at school. Today he is* (look, looked, looking) *for it. I hope John* (find, found, finds) *his hat soon. If he doesn't he will* (felt, feel, feeling) *very sorry. His head will also get wet, because it looks as if it will start* (rain, rained, raining) *before long.*

W O R D   S T R U C T U R E   E X E R C I S E

Verb Endings -ing

Objective

To practice forming the correct verb form from a list of infinitives.

Procedure

Write individual verbs on cards. Use active verbs that can be used in simple sentences (*run, see, wait, throw, hit, go,* etc.). On a piece of paper, write short sentences in which each verb can be used in its various forms: *present, past, present participle* (*I wait, You waited for me, He is waiting on the corner.*). Have your child pick a verb from the stack of cards and then read each sentence, filling in the correct verb form. You can use sentences such as these:

Today I _____. I am _____. Yesterday I _____.
The boy _____.

If your child picked the word run, the sentences would be:

*Today I **run.** I am **running.** Yesterday I **ran.***
*The boy **runs.***

W O R D   S T R U C T U R E   E X E R C I S E

Possessive Endings

Objective

To practice recognizing endings that show ownership.

Procedure

Usually possession is shown by adding -'s to a
singular noun and by adding an apostrophe to a
plural noun (*two cars' radios*). Use sentences such as
the following that involve the idea of ownership. Have
your child tell you which is the right word to use.

This book belongs to the boy. It is the (boys, boy's,
boy) *book.*

*These bicycles belong to the three girls over there.
They are the* (girls, girls', girles) *bicycles.*

That book has a red cover. The (book's, books,
books') *cover is red.*

The river is very high after the rain. The (rivers,
rivers', river's) *current is strong.*

If your child has started learning them in school,
you can also practice possessive pronouns.

This is my book. It is (me, mine, myne).

That book has a green cover. (Its, It's, It) *cover is green.*
(Be sure your child isn't confusing the possessive pronoun *its* with the contraction *it's* which means *it is*.)

You can also give your child a sentence (such as *The
car has a broken window*) and ask the child to reword it
using the possessive form (*The car's window is broken*).

W O R D   S T R U C T U R E   E X E R C I S E

Compound Words

Objective
To practice recognizing the root words included in compound words.

Procedure
Write compound words on individual cards or on a sheet of paper. Ask your child what simple words make up the compound, and why the two words are put together. For example, a *snowman* is a figure of a *man* made of *snow*; a *basketball* is a *ball* thrown through a *basket*. You may use the word list below or other compound words your child can understand.

barefoot	basketball	into
anyone	snowman	upon
upset	sandbox	mailbox
anyway	raincoat	flagpole
without	upstairs	otherwise
daylight	airplane	fingertip
butterfly	everybody	tablecloth
afternoon	sailboat	mousetrap
flashlight	herself	lipstick
anybody	bookcase	sawdust
another	beehive	staircase
fisherman	bedtime	outdoors
because	coffeepot	yourself
battleship	grandmother	housekeeper

WORD STRUCTURE EXERCISE

Compound Words

Objective

To practice forming compound words.

Procedure

Write one part of a compound word on one card and the other part of that compound on another card. Number the paired cards on the back, as shown below.

Some cards may have two or more numbers on the back, because they match more than one card. (*Boat* can also be combined with *sail, tug, motor,* or *speed,* for example.)

Deal out several cards to all players; several children can play or you can play with your child. Each player starts a turn by drawing a card from the hand of the player to his right. The player then lays down any pairs that make compound words. Each match can be checked by seeing if the numbers on the back match as well. The children should keep playing until all of the cards are used up. Whoever forms the most compound words wins.

W O R D   S T R U C T U R E   E X E R C I S E

Compound Words and Imagination

Objective

To practice using compound words in context.

Procedure

Write five or six compound words on a piece of paper, or write individual compound words on cards. Use words that are not related to each other. Your child should pick several of the words and make up a story using all they have chosen. This will call for imagination and a sense of humor. They may choose a group made up of *boxcar, goldfish, grandmother, basketball,* and *beehive,* for example, and will have to play with the words to make up a brief story.

This activity is valuable in a number of ways: it gives your child a chance to use compound words in context; it calls for imagination in the expression of ideas; it requires your child to use phonics skills in spelling; it includes writing practice; and it requires your child to read his own ideas and understand what he reads.

W O R D   S T R U C T U R E   E X E R C I S E

Prefixes

Objective
To practice identifying prefixes in words.

Procedure
On a sheet of paper, write words that have prefixes. You can use the following examples or come up with your own. Read from your list and ask your child for the prefixes in the words. Give words with different prefixes so the exercise isn't too predictable. As an added challenge, you can include words that don't have prefixes so your child won't assume there always will be one to find. Have your child say or underline the prefix in each word.

un-	**re-**	**pre-**
untie	rewrite	precooked
undress	reread	preview
unsafe	return	prepaid
unable	refill	pretend
unpack	recount	preschool

in-	**im-**	**en-**	**ex-**
inactive	impatient	enclose	export
inside	imperfect	enforce	express
inland	impolite	enlarge	exchange
insane	impress	enjoy	exhale

mid-	**dis-**	**mis-**
midnight	displease	misbehave
midday	disconnect	misfortune
midwinter	disagree	misuse
midstream	disobey	misled
midway	dishonest	mistreat

W O R D   S T R U C T U R E   E X E R C I S E

Prefixes

Objective

To practice building new words by adding prefixes to root words.

Procedure

Make a list of prefixes and root words as shown below. The words given in the previous exercise can be used here. Have your child combine each prefix with as many root words as possible. Check words in a dictionary if needed.

Prefixes	**Root Words**
mis-	lay
dis-	tie
re-	please
un-	arm
in-	change
en-	side
ex-	close

Variation

As a game for two or more children, write prefixes and root words on individual cards, and shuffle them together. Deal five cards to each player. Place the deck between the players. The first player draws a card from the deck and, if possible, puts down a pair of cards to form a word. The player uses the word in a sentence, then discards. The next player can pick that card or draw one from the deck. The first player to lay down all of his cards wins.

WORD STRUCTURE EXERCISE

Prefixes — Change Meaning

Objective

To see how prefixes can change the meaning of words.

Procedure

Find articles in newspapers or magazines, making sure each story you pick has some words with prefixes in it. Tell your child to look through the articles for words with prefixes, and to circle those words. Have him explain how the prefixes change the meanings of the words.

W O R D   S T R U C T U R E   E X E R C I S E

Suffixes

Objective
To practice identifying suffixes in words.

Procedure
On a piece of paper, write words that have suffixes. You can use the following examples or come up with your own. Read from your list, and ask your child for the suffixes in the words. Give words with different suffixes so the exercise isn't too predictable. As an added challenge, you can include words that don't have suffixes, so your child won't assume there always will be one to find. Have your child say or underline the suffix in each word.

-less	**-y**	**-ful**	**-en**
careless	rocky	helpful	sweeten
harmless	curly	thankful	soften
cloudless	hilly	playful	woolen
tasteless	sleepy	painful	harden
hopeless	glassy	cupful	ripen

-ion	**-ive**	**-ness**
direction	active	darkness
election	defensive	sadness
perfection	effective	softness
invention	impressive	hardness
attraction	directive	newness

-ly	**-able**	**-ment**	**-ous**
swiftly	lovable	shipment	dangerous
softly	washable	movement	marvelous
quietly	passable	pavement	nervous
neatly	portable	enjoyment	famous
loudly	enjoyable	treatment	humorous

WORD STRUCTURE EXERCISE

Suffixes

Objective

To practice adding the correct suffix to words in context.

Procedure

Write short sentences which include words requiring suffixes. Leave the suffixes out of the sentences, and have your child fill in the blanks where the suffixes are missing. Sentences can vary in difficulty depending on your child's age. In any case, your child should be able to tell from the context what suffix is needed in the blank space. Some examples:

The clerk said the purchase was not return___. (able)

The team showed good sportsman___. (ship)

Do not be care___ when using electricity. (less)

The gray skies made the day very gloom__. (y)

The birds flew swift__ through the sky. (ly)

The team was in a cheer___ mood after winning the game. (ful)

W O R D   S T R U C T U R E   E X E R C I S E

Root Words

Objective

To practice identifying root words when prefixes and suffixes are present.

Procedure

Write a list of words that contain prefixes and suffixes. Ask your child either to say or write down the root word. Many words ending with suffixes can be changed by adding prefixes such as *in-*, *un-*, *dis-*, *non-* to the beginning of the word. It's possible to change many words starting with prefixes by attaching *-able*, *-ly*, *-ous*, etc., to the end of the word. Some examples:

incompletely	*complete*
disorderly	_____
nonpoisonous	_____
dislocated	_____
unbreakable	_____
refillable	_____
removable	_____
disagreement	_____
uncomfortable	_____
inactive	_____
unhealthy	_____
inexpensive	_____
undependable	_____
ineffective	_____
unavailable	_____

W O R D   S T R U C T U R E   E X E R C I S E

Contractions

Objective

To practice recognizing contractions and the pairs of words that form them.

Procedure

Write each contraction on a separate card and the pair of words that create it on another card. Use the examples given below, or any other combinations you want. Place several of the word pairs in a column on the left, and contraction cards in a different order in a column on the right. Your child should try to figure out which word pairs make which contraction. You can also show your child the card with the contraction, and ask for the pair of words that form it.

did not—didn't	we have—we've
was not—wasn't	can not—can't
he is—he's	is not—isn't
you are—you're	I will—I'll
does not—doesn't	I am—I'm
has not—hasn't	he will—he'll
she is—she's	it is—it's
had not—hadn't	have not—haven't
they are—they're	they have—they've
they would—they'd	there is—there's
we are—we're	do not—don't
we will—we'll	she will—she'll
I have—I've	should not—shouldn't

WORD STRUCTURE EXERCISE

Contractions

Objective
   To practice using contractions in context.

Procedure
   On individual cards, print sentences using groups of words that can be combined to form contractions. Use examples from the previous exercise, or any others you choose. On separate cards, write the contractions that fit into those sentences. Make sure there are as many contraction cards as sentence cards; if you use the contraction *can't* in three different sentences, make three different cards that say *can't*. Show your child the sentence cards one at a time, and have the child find the correct contraction card for each sentence. Keep going until all the contraction cards are used. The cards should look like this:

I CAN NOT FIND MY SHOE.

CAN'T

Variation
   As a game for two or more children, shuffle all the cards together and deal out five to each player. Place the rest of the cards in the middle of the playing area. The first player draws a card, and if it makes a pair, he lays down the pair, and the next player takes a turn. The winner is the first to lay down all of his cards.

Summary

There are steps that a child can follow to find the meaning of an unfamiliar word. The steps include looking at the context, the first and last sounds in the word, and the link between how the word is spelled and how it sounds. Think about both the appearance and sound of a word in trying to discover what the word is. Learn how prefixes, suffixes, contractions and other changes in words can affect word meanings. Break an unfamiliar word into its parts to help figure out what the word is and what it means.

Chapter Five

Building a strong vocabulary

A word fitly spoken is like apples
of gold in a setting of silver.
—Proverbs 23:11

Vocabulary is such an important part of school
and business success that some psychologists use it as a measure of intelligence or of
subject knowledge. To get a quick estimate, for instance, of your child's knowledge of our federal government, give him a list of words and ask him to define
them or match them to a list of definitions. Take these
words, for example:

Constitution	Congress
Bill of Rights	Supreme Court
Executive branch	House of Representatives
Cabinet officers	Balance of power
States' rights	

The ease and accuracy with which he defines these
terms would give you a strong sense of his knowledge
of civics or of a social studies course on our federal
government. Why? Because words represent the ideas
in our minds. Most of our thinking is done with words.

Therefore, in a real sense, by increasing our vocabulary we are increasing our storehouse of ideas. We are increasing our ability to link one item to another, that is, our potential for complex thinking.

As your children move through their early years in school, you should of course help them deal with all the new words they encounter and help them tie these new words to ideas they already know. In health, for instance, they will hear and read about *hygiene*, *bacteria*, and *viruses*. Many families tell their children that they have to wash their hands so they don't catch *germs* (or *bugs*). By tying the scientific terms to concepts the child already has, you make vocabulary growth easier and more natural.

Reading vocabulary

A general speaking or listening vocabulary is the basis for a reading vocabulary. There is a distinction between a listening vocabulary and a reading vocabulary. There is an act of visual recognition in reading that is a learned habit. A reading vocabulary, therefore, is that body of printed words that a person recognizes quickly and reads fluently. In the early years of school, a child's reading vocabulary is limited by his reading practice and by his ability to see the connection between printed words and the words in his listening/speaking vocabulary.

You should always be alert for opportunities to enlarge your children's general vocabulary. You should also help them expand their reading vocabulary by encouraging frequent reading and by helping them recognize in print those words that are already in their speaking vocabulary.

Building a broad vocabulary is one of the most valuable things you can do for your child. The larger your child's vocabulary, the more likely he or she is to succeed. That does not mean you should take a list of words and have your child look up dictionary definitions. Rather, vocabulary should come from all the natural situations you encounter: ads, newspaper headlines, listening to discussions, reading aloud. When you see or hear an interesting word, talk about it with your child. Discovering words and their meanings can be a game the entire family will enjoy.

Sight words

Just as you build a large speaking vocabulary through curiosity and discussion, so do you build a large reading vocabulary. With your child, keep vocabulary development informal and as natural as possible.

There are many words that come up so often in reading that everyone learns them as word units: for example, *stop, McDonald's, boy, girl* and so on. By the time a child starts the first grade, he usually has a significant vocabulary of these so-called "sight words." With young children, point out the words you see as you drive or walk and help them develop this storehouse of words. It will later serve as a basis for fluent reading.

It is of course true that your child must learn to "sound out" some new words as they come up in reading, but it's also worth noting that a good number of common words can be dealt with more easily as whole words. Experienced readers don't stop and sound out every word they face in print; this is not only unnecessary, but undesirable, because it blocks understanding and quickly makes reading very boring. Furthermore, many of the most common English words—*the, when,* and *how*—are easier to learn by sight.

It probably won't surprise you to find that *a, and, I, the, to,* and *you* are the most common words in children's books. Almost as frequent are *have, in, is, it, my, of, was,* and *we.* These words, together with verbs such as *run, see,* and *walk,* form some of the simplest sentences that can be written in English.

The following words are used very frequently in children's books.

about	had	said
after	has	saw
all	he	school
am	here	see
an	him	she
are	his	some
as	home	
at	house	that
	how	their
back		them
be	if	then
because		there
but	just	they
by		this
	like	time
came	little	
can		up
come	made	us
	me	
day	mother	very
dear		
did	not	well
do	now	went
down		were
	on	what
for	one	when
friend	our	will
from	out	with
	over	would
get		write
go	play	
going	put	your
good		
got		

These and other frequently used words form the nucleus of a reading vocabulary. Make your young child aware of their use in signs, ads, headlines, and stories that you read to him. You may want to expand on this list by teaching the written names of common household objects: *chair, table, lamp, bowl, dish, spoon, fork, cat, dog,* and so on. You can make a game from labels that you place on common objects. Other words can be taught as they relate to things that are encountered outside the home: *car, bus, flag, house, school, room, desk,* and so on.

Techniques for learning vocabulary while reading

There are several ways to help a child learn vocabulary while reading. Use those methods that seem to work best.

➡ **Meaning.** Children learn whole words by linking the words with what they mean. Therefore, practice words in sentences that help make their meanings clear. This is especially desirable when words are fairly abstract, such as a pronoun that refers back to something already introduced:

"The *book* has many pictures.

It is very interesting."

"*John* is very helpful at home.

He takes out the garbage and mows the lawn."

You can also practice the meaning of active verbs by playing charades; children like to act out the meaning of written words such as *run, jump, throw,* and *catch.* This can also be done with some nouns, where your child can imitate the sound a *cat, dog,* or *cow* makes.

➡ **Picture association.** Practice connecting written words with matching pictures. Cut out pictures from magazines and paste them onto cards. You can then either print the names of the pictures on the back or make up a separate set of cards with the words on them.

➡ **Shape.** Sometimes a child can remember a word by thinking about how it is shaped. It might help here to tell your child to draw a line around the letters in the words (especially those that may be difficult) to highlight the visual features of these words. Use this technique sparingly, and only when you think it is worth focusing attention on the word's shape.

dog   mother   elephant

➡ **Writing association.** By actually writing it down, your child may be better able to remember a word. If your son or daughter can't write yet, just tracing the letters with their finger can be worthwhile. Encourage writing and copying sentences because it reinforces the connection between the message and its printed form.

Listed in Appendix D are words used in one first-grade reading program. This list is attached as a point of reference so you can get an idea of the kind of reading vocabulary you can expect your child to develop during the first grade. Other reading books' vocabulary may be slightly different, but all of them will emphasize the most common words.

These words are not to be memorized as words in a list. They will be learned usually through frequent reading. But if your child continues to stumble over these or similar common words, then you should pull those words out for individual study. Write problem words on a separate sheet or on a card to discuss them, to identify their sound-symbol relations, or to find other ways to make them easier to recognize in the future. The objective is to enable your child to read high-frequency words quickly so they don't prevent him from understanding the message.

Techniques for expanding vocabulary

Most children are interested in words. They hear new ones and try them out and they come to realize that words are power, that an increased vocabulary is a sign of maturity. It is also a sign of success in school and in the business world. Though a large vocabulary does not guarantee success, many studies show that high achievers in school and in business have much larger vocabularies than those who have average or below-average achievement. So it is certainly worth the effort to try deliberately to expand your child's vocabulary.

Word for today

Encourage your child to expand his vocabulary by setting up a "word for today" routine. For example, you might say, "*Astronomy* is the study of the stars and planets in the universe. Can you use it in a sentence?" Prompt your child to look at a new word and use his word-attack skills to fix it in memory. "How many syllables are in the word? How does each syllable sound? What other words can you think of that start the same way?" (*Astronaut* and *astronomer* are two examples.) This helps the child recognize the word for reading, and it opens up the opportunity to make the word for today grow into several words each day.

It's a good idea to put the daily word in a notebook or on a bulletin board. Each day, a new word can be discussed and put on the board, perhaps with its definition and a sentence using the word. Across one year, learning only one new word each day will expand your child's vocabulary significantly and will improve his chances for success in school.

Vocabulary development: A continuous process

Vocabulary building and related activities shouldn't end with primary school. Learning new words becomes all the more important in the later grades as subjects become more and more complicated. From the early grades all the way through high school, children should see word power as an important part of their growth because each new word actually represents a new idea.

Young children need to be involved as directly as possible with what they're learning in the stories they read in order to make the words and ideas as vivid as possible. As your child takes trips to museums, libraries and zoos, for example, it's helpful to do experiments and projects, make models, and so on. In taking part in an experiment dealing with the speed and direction of the wind, your child is exposed to words dealing with the subject, and discusses terms such as *direction, pressure* and *measure*.

Each new idea represents more competence and more confidence in what you know.

A new experience alone is not enough to build a child's vocabulary. Your child could go to a zoo or museum and not pick up a single new word there. Someone needs to introduce, define, and discuss words related to the child's vocabulary. Then those words need to be used often enough to make them a regular part of his vocabulary. You are the logical person to expand your child's experiences by using more precise terms and explanations. Those are not all monkeys in this section of the zoo; they are gorillas, chimpanzees, orangutans, baboons, and so on. New vocabulary arises from daily life—the newspaper, television, school textbooks, trips to the mall. Be a learner along with your child. Help each other grow by sharing new words and new ideas with each other.

An excellent way to build vocabulary is to read a wide variety of material. New words from different fields are learned then, as are new meanings for familiar words. For example, a child reading a book about old sailing ships may learn the word **galleon**, and also learn that **league** can mean a measurement (approximately six feet) as well as a group of sports teams.

Your child can also build his vocabulary by looking for and using *figures of speech*, that is, colorful expressions that represent life but are not meant to be read literally. "She was crushed by his actions" does not mean that the lady was smashed down and broken apart. But the image of "crushing" shows how badly damaged her spirits were because of his actions. This valuable alternative vocabulary adds definition and refinement to meaning. In sentences in which figures of speech appear, the expressions have to be understood before the sentences make any sense:

- His face fell.
- Don't throw away your money on that.
- She was bursting with pride.
- His eyes lit up with anticipation.

Another way to build vocabulary is by looking for synonyms, antonyms and homonyms. Synonyms are words that mean the same thing (*big* and *large*), antonyms are words that are opposites (*hot* and *cold*, *up* and *down*), and homonyms are words that sound the same but are different in both spelling and meaning (*here* and *hear*, *wait* and *weight*).

The exercises on the following pages deal with vocabulary building. They offer a variety of methods you can use for assisting your child in learning new words.

Vocabulary Exercise
A Pile of Words

Procedure

Have your child write a new or interesting word on a card. When he child is able to recognize the word and use it in a sentence, the word can be put into a stack marked "Words I Know." Challenge your child to add at least one new word to the stack each day. Review the cards in the stack from time to time; any words that are forgotten can be taken out of the stack and studied until they are learned.

Variation

Even the more advanced readers can use this activity as a way of increasing vocabulary. Along with asking an older child to say the word and use it in a sentence, you can ask for synonyms and antonyms.

Vocabulary Exercise
Crossword Puzzles

Procedure

Show how a crossword puzzle works and talk about how to put one together. You and your child can make your own simple puzzle. Later, he can come up with his own based on a familiar theme such as a favorite sport, season of the year, or the characters and events in a story. Two children could each make their own crossword puzzles and them swap and solve them. With a younger child (in the first grade or in the second grade), it's probably best to provide a puzzle. The child can build on word squares and clues using what you've done as a starting point.

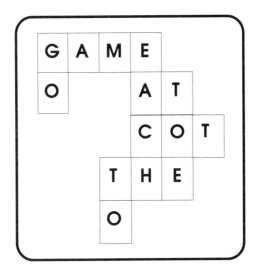

Variation

More advanced readers could try the crossword puzzles found in newspapers or puzzle books. Children can work together on harder puzzles.

Vocabulary Exercise
Synonym Rummy

Procedure
Write pairs of synonyms, putting each word on a separate card. The list below can be used for this and other exercises involving synonyms. Give your child several word cards. (For a very young child, you may want to deal out no more than four or five cards at a time.) Have him pick from the stack of remaining cards and try to match the word drawn from the stack with one of the cards in his hand. As the child matches synonyms, the pairs are laid down, and he keeps drawing new cards until all of them are matched.

Variation
As a game for two or more children, you can shuffle all of the cards together and deal out five to each player. The first player draws from the stack of remaining cards and discards any synonym pairs. Each player follows the same routine; the first player to discard all of his cards wins.

pick—gather	slim—thin	gigantic—huge
cut—chop	gloomy—dark	pledge—promise
clear—plain	mistake—error	voyage—journey
buy—purchase	remember—recall	miniature—small
ring—circle	strength—power	fair—just
large—huge	accuse—blame	serious—grave
jump—leap	reason—cause	scare—frighten
fall—tumble	relate—tell	happy—glad
permit—allow	parcel—package	many—numerous
quiet—noiseless	loyal—faithful	expand—enlarge
slide—skid	grateful—thankful	rescue—save
select—choose	anxious—eager	evil—wicked
old—ancient	conquer—defeat	port—harbor
forever—always	sadness—grief	smooth—even
empty—vacant	tired—weary	

Vocabulary Exercise
Synonym Spin

Procedure

Make a large spinner from cardboard, using the illustration below as a guide. Draw a circle in the middle of the spinner, then another outside that one. Divide the spinner into sections (like pie slices), and print words within the sections. Make a pointer out of cardboard and attach it to the circle with a brass paper fastener. In the outer circle, use words that have fairly obvious synonyms. The second circle should contain words whose synonyms are not quite so obvious, and the innermost circle should be as challenging as possible for your child's age. On a separate card list synonyms that could work.

Any number of children can play this game. Each player spins, and gives a synonym for each word on which the spinner comes to

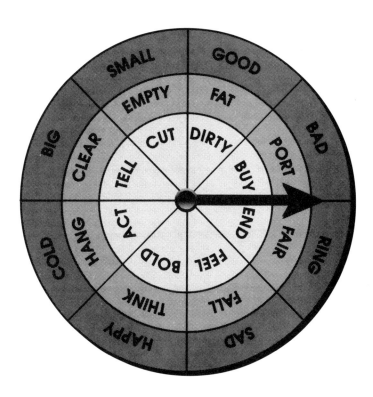

rest, starting with the word in the outer circle and moving toward the center. For each correct answer, the player gets two points for giving a synonym for the word in the outer circle, 3 for the middle circle, and 5 for the inner one. Each player records his synonyms and points on a tally sheet. A child playing alone can try to improve his score with each round. Any missed words can be worked on independently. Similar games can be played with antonyms, homonyms or general definitions. Keep a synonym dictionary handy for answering questions.

Vocabulary Exercise
Synonym Bingo

Procedure
Make a bingo board with squares marked off; small cards, each one with a word on it, can be placed on the squares, so the board itself can be reused. Print synonyms on other cards and use them for calling the game. As each word is called, the player must find its synonym on the board and then remove that word card and keep it. The game continues until all cards are removed from the board. If two or more children are playing, the winner is the one with the most cards when the board is cleared.

PLAY	CUT	BUY	SLIDE
SLIM	FALL	JUMP	RING
OLD	LARGE	QUIET	PENNY
CLEAN	TELL	CAUSE	POWER

You may want to use a synonym dictionary to construct this game. Here are synonyms to match the list above.

enjoy	slice	purchase	slip
thin	stumble	leap	circle
ancient	big	silent	cent
cleanse	report	produce	authority

Vocabulary Exercise
Find the Synonyms

Procedure

Write a series of five or six words, with two of the words being synonyms. The other words should be clearly different so there can be no confusion:

grasp   drop   run   **hold**   forget   see

calm   angry   happy   green   upset

Have your child say or underline the two words in each group that are synonyms. Make sure that you don't always begin the series of words with one of the synonyms.

For young children, you can make the exercise easier by giving one word and having them pick its synonym from among three or four choices:

small: happy   tiny   calm   cold

fast: sleepy   quick   red

Variation

Ask your child to construct a series of these word sets and give them to you to figure out. A synonym dictionary would be a great help for both of you.

Vocabulary Exercise
Antonyms

Procedure

The previous exercises dealing with synonyms can easily by adapted for practicing antonyms. The following list provides a number of antonyms to use for the exercises.

come—go	poor—rich	ask—answer
summer—winter	cool—warm	hot—cold
forward—backward	old—young	day—night
strong—weak	dirty—clean	quiet—noisy
above—below	stop—start	arrive—depart
stop—start	arrive—depart	straight—crooked
deep—shallow	absent—present	little—big
width—length	pretty—ugly	high—low
sweet—sour	soft—hard	quick—slow
worst—best	burn—freeze	waken—sleep
graceful—awkward	freeze—thaw	quit—continue
mind—disobey	exit—entrance	scarce—plentiful
solid—liquid	cry—laugh	loose—tight
seldom—often	true—false	ancient—modern
strange—familiar	appear—vanish	smooth—rough
hungry—full	wealth—poverty	careful—careless
happiness—sorrow	remember—forget	calm—stormy
proud—humble	hate—love	dull—sharp
find—lose	tough—tender	sad—cheerful
polite—rude		

Many synonym dictionaries also give antonyms as part of each citation. Synonym dictionaries can be found in your local bookstores.

Vocabulary Exercise
Homonyms—Words that sound the same

Procedure

The previous exercises dealing with synonyms can be adapted to work with homonyms. The list below offers a number of homonyms that can be used in these exercises. In all work with homonyms, it's necessary for the child to spell and define the two differently spelled words which are pronounced the same way. It also helps to have your child use the two words in sentences to underscore their different meanings:

> *We can not see the* **sun** *on a cloudy day.*
> *Mr. Jones and his* **son** *were at the game.*

so—sew	not—knot	son—sun
know—no	beat—beet	sale—sail
too—to—two	weak—week	blew—blue
forth—fourth	pair—pear	four—for
maid—made	one—won	would—wood
peace—piece	do—due—dew	buy—by
deer—dear	here—hear	vein—vain
meat—meet	waist—waste	mail—male
road—rode	hole-whole	tide—tied
nights—knights	lead—led	knew—new
their—there	sea—see	fair—fare
steel—steal	pane—pain	rap—wrap
wait—weight	ate—eight	tail—tale
hair—hare	our—hour	some—sum
rains—reins	heard—herd	aisle—isle
threw—through	beech—beach	bear—bare
guest—guessed	fowl—foul	

Vocabulary Exercise

Figures of Speech

Procedures

> *When Ginny was praised, she blossomed like a flower.*
> *The clouds of sadness lifted from her eyes and her smile*
> *spread sunshine around the room.*

These two sentences are filled with figures of speech. Ginny did not actually blossom. She changed from a sad person to a happy person. You can help your child understand figurative language by using pictures or cartoons that can be matched with a figurative expression. On a separate card write the expression that goes with each picture. Once you show your child each picture, have the child find the expression card that matches. For example, a picture of a cat slinking through tall grass might suggest the sentence "This cat is as sly as a fox," and a picture of a sick man in bed suggests "The old man was under the weather." Eventually you may have your child make up figures of speech that match the pictures. Here are a few examples:

"He is as mad as a wet hen!"

"He really threw himself into his work."

"They are chewing the fat."

You can lead your child to understand the expression by asking a series of questions about the pictures: "What are the two men doing?" (Arguing.) "Is he having a quiet discussion?" (No, he look upsets and angry.) If you dunked a chicken in a bucket of water, how would the chicken act? (Wild clucking.) "What's another way to say he looks angry?" (He's as mad as a wet hen.)

Some children's books, such as *Amelia Bedelia*, show what happens when book characters try to interpret figurative language in a literal way. Reading those books together can be as much fun as a barrel of monkeys.

Chapter Six

The value of reading aloud

It is even better the second time—in literature.
The children understand this well when they ask for
the same story over and over again.
—*C.S. Lewis*

If you want to show your children that books are important, then you have to let them see you read. If you want to demonstrate that books are interesting and fun, then you should try reading aloud to your children.

Among the various approaches to reading, reading aloud most nearly resembles our most common form of communication: person to person conversation. This makes reading aloud particularly attractive to many people. It can take on the closeness and the sense of intimacy that you can achieve when two people talk face to face.

For very young children there is an obvious advantage. They may have not yet figured out the print code, but when their parents read aloud to them, they can participate in the excitement or the humor of a book. Later, in their school years, children still appreciate hearing a story read to them, probably because it represents a form of togetherness that is reassuring.

Once children can read on their own, they can be readers as well as listeners. When they do their share of the reading, you can model the behavior of a good listener. You can ask questions for clarification; you can ask for a passage to be read again because you liked it or because you need another reading in order to understand it more fully; or you can make a comment that emphasizes the ideas or the language of the story. Reactions such as these help to create the atmosphere of a conversation. You and the reader are beginning a kind of dialog over the book you are reading. Then, when it is your turn to read aloud, your children will feel more comfortable about stating their reactions or asking the questions that come to their minds as you read.

Is there a continuing value in reading aloud to children, even when they are older?

If you think about what makes a story comprehensible to you, those are the things that you should try to talk about when you or your children are reading aloud. Some of the common techniques for comprehending are:

- **visualizing**—"What a vivid picture that paints in my mind."
- **making it personal**—"I felt that way when my grandmother died."
- **taking a character's point of view**—"If I were in her shoes, . . ."
- **predicting outcomes**—"I'll bet she's going to catch him when he tries to run away from home."

Take a conversational tone

Some people read aloud better than others. Some people run or play golf better than others. In each of these skills there is a matter of natural talent. But more important is the question of practice. If you want to become a better golfer, you have to practice. If you want to become a better reader, you have to practice. The best time to practice is when your child is young. Then, when he expects a better performance, you will have had several years of practice that have made you better.

You talk all the time. The way you talk seems to serve you, to hold the interest of those around you. Use your conversational tone when you read. In conversation you change your voice to express surprise, anger, sadness, mystery. Do the same thing when you read. That's all your children expect of you—that you sound like you are talking to them. If you feel uncomfortable at first, there are ways that you can get some help. One of the easiest is to borrow a tape-recorded book from the library or purchase one from your local bookstore. By listening to others read a book aloud, you can find some pointers that will help you.

In Appendix C of this book there is a short list of audio books for children. You might want to listen to one or more of them as you drive or as you jog.

After you hear others read a children's book, you will gain a sense of how you might read to your children. Keep the story moving at a steady pace, as clear as you can make it. Let your voice reflect the

interest you have in the story and in the benefits your children get from listening to and responding to a story.

Good literature gives perspective

We all can vividly remember that favorite teacher who would read aloud to the entire class every day after lunch. Our images of particular characters such as Tom Sawyer or Pippi Longstocking remained with us long after the book was finished. Those books have remained our lifelong friends.

As parents, we read aloud to our children to provide a similar experience for them. But reading aloud not only establishes a special time for sharing, it also affects our understanding of language.

We read to children for many of the reasons that we talk to them. We want to explain and provide information about the world. We want them to be curious and inquisitive and see language as entertaining and stimulating.

Reading aloud affects our children's reading competencies in important ways. When students hear a story, they often are motivated to read it themselves. It stimulates and expands their interests and appreciation of certain types of literature.

Good literature gives children a perspective that enables them to evaluate the books they read by themselves. Their comprehension also improves as their vocabulary and information about the world (their background knowledge for reading other material) expand.

Reading aloud affects the full range of language processes. It helps children discover similarities and differences between oral and written language, sharpening their speaking and listening skills and their understanding of narrative structure. Writing is affected positively because reading aloud provides them with opportunities to use their imagination and exposes them to different literary styles. They may try out these styles in their own writing.

While reading aloud improves reading and listening skills and expands use of oral language, it also motivates children to read. We know that children who have been read to at home usually like to read and therefore become proficient readers.

Make reading aloud interactive

Just as you probably talk to yourself about the things that you read, so you want to talk with your children when you are reading aloud or when they are reading aloud to you. You ask yourself whether or not a statement is believable, what is going to happen next, and how these ideas apply to your life. Those are natural reactions as your mind interacts with the mind of the writer.

Encourage your children to interact with the book by talking aloud to yourself or by asking them about their own feelings and thoughts as you move through the story. You are modelling thinking and problem-solving for them, but it will seem so natural that they will not see your comments and your questions as interfering with the story. If you overdo that sort of self-talk and questioning, chances are they will let you know.

The advantage of self-talk while reading is that it helps you understand.

Here are examples of the kinds of questions and statements that you might use as you read aloud or listen to your child read to you:

- Has anything like this ever happened to you?
- Do you think you felt the same as the story characters?
- I can see that event so clearly in my mind that it is like watching TV.
- I am surprised at what he said. Does it surprise you?

- Which character interests you the most?
- Is there anything in this book that you would tell your friends about?

The point is that you want to talk about the story as it progresses and talk about it as naturally as possible. Your thoughts and those of your children will make book discussions a natural part of your lives. As your child gets older, you may find that these book talks are valuable ways for you to maintain communication with your children. After all, when you are talking about the characters and the events in a book, you are not digging into the personal lives of your children. You are talking about a life outside the intimate parent-child relationship.

Choose a book and do it

Reading aloud can be a pleasure to you and your children, and we know that it is beneficial to them in school and in the general experiences that reading aloud provides. So find a book and begin.

In the remaining pages of this chapter we have listed books for children by age and by the types of literature that children often like. You will recognize some of them, and some of them will be new to you. These books were chosen because they lend themselves to being read aloud.

The books listed in this chapter have been recommended by at least three people who have studied read-aloud books. In Appendix E you will find a list of resources for parents. These are the resources that we used in selecting books for this chapter. For more information on read-aloud books, consult one of the resources listed in the appendix or ask your librarian for help.

Read-Aloud Book List

Preschool

These preschool books enable you and your child to sit together and explore the story and the pictures. They are listed according to broad themes to help you choose books that may illustrate something that is currently important in your family.

Sharing with Friends

Ancona, George. *Getting Together.*
Cohen, Miriam. *Will I Have a Friend?*
Gretz, Susanna. *Frog in the Middle.*
Heine, Helme. *Friends.*
Johnson, Delores. *What Will Mommy Do When I'm At School?*
Simon, Nora. *I'm Busy, Too.*

Speak and Listen

Aylesworth, Jim. *Country Crossing.*
Hautzig, Ester. *In the Park.*
Kamen. Gloria. *Paddle, Said the Swan.*
Keats, Ezra Jack. *Apt. 3.*
Schlein, Miriam. *Big Talk.*
Serfozo, Mary. *Rain Talk.*

Paint and Build

Browne, Anthony. *The Little Bear Book.*
Hoban, Tana. *circles, triangles and squares.*
————. *Read Signs.*
Hutchins, Pat. *Changes, Changes.*
Jonas, Ann. *Round Trip.*
Serfozo, Mary. *Who Said Red?*

Eat Well

Gross, Ruth Belov. *What's on My Plate?*
Morris, Ann. *Bread, Bread, Bread.*
Sharmat, Mitchell. *Gregory, the Terrible Eater.*

Sing and Dance Away!

Isadora, Rachel. *Max.*
Langstaff, John. *Oh, A-Hunting We Will Go.*
Sage, James. *The Little Band.*

Animal Friends

Allen, Majorie and Shelley Rotner. *Changes.*
deRegniers, Beatrice Schenck. *May I Bring a Friend.*
Domanska, Janina. *Little Red Hen.*
————. *What Do You See?*
Hutchins, Pat. *Good-Night Owl.*
————. *Rosie's Walk.*
Keats, Ezra Jack. *Hi, Cat!*
————. *Kitten for a Day.*
————. *Pet Show.*
Reeves, Mona Rabun. *I Had a Cat.*

Tales of Wonder

Ancona, G. and M. Beth. *Handtalk Zoo.*
Brown, Marcia. *Stone Soup.*
Dragonwagon, Cresent. *Half a Moon and One Whole Star.*
Greeley, Valerie. *White Is the Moon.*
Jones, Maurice. *I'm Going on a Dragon Hunt.*
Takeshita, Fumiko. *The Park Bench.*

Personal Growth

Geraghty, Paul. *Look Out, Patrick.*
Hartman, Gail. *As the Crow Flies.*
Howard, Elizabeth F. *The Train to Lulu's.*
Roe, Eileen. *All I Am.*
———. *With My Brother/Con mi Hermano.*
Wynne-Jones, Tim. *Builder of the Moon.*

Kindergarten — Sixth Grade

These books have been recommended in at least three sources of read-aloud books for children.

Adventure, K–3

Bemelmans, Ludwig. *Madeline.*
Cooney, Barbara. *Miss Rumphius.*
Grimm, Jacob. *Bremen Town Musicians.*
Noble, Trinka H. *The Day Jimmy's Boa Ate the Wash.*
Peet, Bill. *Chester the Worldly Pig.*
Sendak, Maurice. *Where the Wild Things Are.*
Smith, Robert K. *Chocolate Fever.*
Steig, William. *Solomon the Rusty Nail.*
Swallow, Pam. *Melvil and Dewey in the Chips.*
Warner, Gertrude C. *Boxcar Children.*

Adventure, 4–6

Cleary, Beverly. *The Mouse and the Motorcycle.*
Clemens, Samuel. *The Adventures of Huckleberry Finn.*
———. *The Adventures of Tom Sawyer.*
Collodi, Carlo. *The Adventures of Pinocchio.*
DuBois, William P. *The Twenty-one Balloons.*
Fitzgerald, John. *The Great Brain.*
Fleischman, Sid. *Humbug Mountain.*

————. *The Whipping Boy.*

Pyle, Howard. *The Story of King Arthur and His Knights.*

Selden, George. *The Cricket in Times Square.*

Sperry, Armstrong. *Call It Courage.*

Steig, William. *Abel's Island.*

Stevenson, Robert Louis. *Treasure Island.*

Animals, K–3

Barrett, Judi. *Animals Should Definitely Not Wear Clothing.*

Farley, Walter. *Black Stallion.*

Lofting, Hugh. *The Story of Doctor Doolittle.*

McCloskey, Robert. *Make Way for Ducklings.*

Milne, A. A. *Winnie-the-Pooh.*

Potter, Beatrix. *The Tale of Peter Rabbit.*

Simon, Seymour. *Animal Fact, Animal Fable.*

Slobodkina, Esphyr. *Caps for Sale.*

Suess, Dr. *Horton Hatches the Egg.*

Titus, Eve. *Anatole.*

Ungerer, Tomi. *Crictor.*

White, E. B. *Charlotte's Web.*

Animals, 4–6

Alexander, Lloyd. *The Town Cats and Other Tales.*

Armstrong, William. *Sounder.*

Bond, Michael. *A Bear Called Paddington.*

Burnford, Sheila. *Incredible Journey.*

Garfield, James. *Follow My Leader.*

Heath, W. L. *Max the Great.*

Herriot, James. *Blossom Comes Home.*

Holland, Isabella. *Alan and the Animal Kingdom.*

King-Smith, Dick. *Harry's Mad.*

Morey, Walt. *Gentle Ben.*

Fantasy, K–3

Balian, Lorna. *The Animal.*
Banks, Lynne Reid. *Indian in the Cupboard.*
Faulkner, Matt. *The Amazing Voyage of Jackie Grace.*
Gerstein, Mordecai. *Arnold of the Ducks.*
Kellogg, Steven. *Island of the Skog.*
Lionni, Leo. *Frederick.*
Peet, Bill. *Whingdingdilly.*
Sadler, Marilyn. *Alistair in Outer Space.*
Seeger, Pete. *Abiyoyo.*
Seuss, Dr. *And to Think that I Saw It on Mulberry Street.*
Van Woerkom, Dorothy. *Alexander and the Rockeater.*
Yorinks, Arthur. *Company's Coming.*
———. *It Happened in Pinsk.*

Fantasy, 4–6

Alexander, Lloyd. *The Book of Three.*
———. *Westmark.*
Ames, Mildred. *Is There Life on a Plastic Planet?*
Avi. *Bright Shadow.*
Babbitt, Natalie. *The Search for Delicious.*
———. *Tuck Everlasting.*
Baum, Frank L. *Ozma of Oz.*
Cameron, Eleanor. *Wonderful Flight to the Mushroom Planet.*
Carroll, Lewis. *Alice's Adventures in Wonderland.*
Dahl, Roald. *James and the Giant Peach.*
Grahame, Kenneth. *The Wind in the Willows.*
LeGuin, Ursula. *A Wizard of Earthsea.*
L'Engle, Madeleine. *A Wrinkle in Time.*
Lewis, C. S. *The Lion, the Witch, and the Wardrobe.*
Norton, Mary. *The Borrowers.*

O'Brien, Robert. *Mrs. Frisby and the Rats of NIMH.*
Pinkwater, Daniel. *Lizard Music.*
Schwartz, Alvin. *Scary Stories to Tell in the Dark.*
Sleator, William. *Into the Dream.*
Slote, Alfred. *My Trip to Alpha.*
Tolkien, J. R. R. *The Hobbit.*
White, E. B. *The Trumpet of the Swan.*

Folk & Fairy Tales, K–3

Aardema, Verna. *Bringing the Rain to Kapiti Plain.*
———. *Why Mosquitoes Buzz in People's Ears.*
Aesop. *Seven Fables from Aesop.*
Andersen, Hans Christian. *The Emperor's New Clothes.*
Brown, Marcia. *Three Billy Goats Gruff.*
Cooney, Barbara. *Chanticleer and the Fox.*
Emberley, Barbara. *One Wide River to Cross.*
Haley, Gail. *A Story, a Story: An African Tale.*
Hyman, Trina Schart. *Little Red Riding Hood.*
Kipling, Rudyard. *Elephant's Child.*
———. *How the Camel Got His Hump.*
McDermott, Gerald. *Anansi the Spider: A Tale from the Ashanti.*
———. *The Stonecutter: A Japanese Tale.*
Mosel, Arlene. *Tikki Tikki Tembo.*
Perrault, Charles. *Puss in Boots.*
Wildsmith, Brian. *The Lion and the Rat.*
Zemach, Harve. *Nail Soup: A Swedish Folk Tale.*
Zemach, Margot. *It Could Always Be Worse.*

Folk & Fairy Tales, 4–6

Asbjornsen, Peter C. *East O' the Sun and West O' the Moon: An Old Norse Tale.*
Chase, Richard. *Jack Tales.*
Goble, Paul. *Buffalo Woman.*

Hamilton, Virginia. *The People Could Fly: American Black Folktales.*

Kha, Dang Manh. *In the Land of Small Dragon: A Vietnamese Folktale.*

Lester, Julius. *How Many Spots Does a Leopard Have?: And Other Tales.*

Phelps, Ethel Johnston. *The Maid of the North and Other Folk Tale Heroines.*

Schwartz, Alvin. *Whoppers: Tall Tales and Other Lies.*

Singer, Isaac Bashevis. *Zlateh the Goat and Other Stories.*

Uchida, Yoshiko. *Sea of Gold and Other Tales from Japan.*

Historical Fiction, K–3

Cohen, Barbara. *Molly's Pilgrim.*
———. *Thank You, Jackie Robinson.*
Dalgliesh, Alice. *The Courage of Sarah Noble.*
Gauch, Patricia Lee. *This Time, Tempe Wick?*
Hall, Donald. *Ox-cart Man.*
Kellogg, Steven. *Johnny Appleseed.*
Lord, Bett Bao. *In the Year of the Boar and Jackie Robinson.*
Monjo, F. N. *The Drinking Gourd.*
Polacco, Patricia. *The Keeping Quilt.*
Snyder, Carol. *Ike and Mama and the Once-a-Year Suit.*
Turkle, Brinton. *Adventures of Obadiah.*
Wilder, Laura Ingalls. *Little House in the Big Woods.*

Historical Fiction, 4–6

Brink, Carol R. *Caddie Woodlawn.*
Burch, Robert. *Ida Comes Early Over the Mountain.*
Coerr, Eleanor. *Sadako & the Thousand Paper Cranes.*

Collier, James. *My Brother Sam is Dead.*
Cooney, Barbara. *Island Boy.*
Fleischman, Sid. *By the Great Horn Spoon.*
Fritz, Jean. *And Then What Happened, Paul Revere?*
———. *What's the Big Idea, Ben Franklin?*
———. *Where Do You Think You're Going,*
    Christopher Columbus?
MacLachlan, Patricia. *Sarah, Plain and Tall.*
O'Dell, Scott. *Island of the Blue Dolphins.*
Speare, Elizabeth George. *Sign of the Beaver.*
Taylor, Sydney. *All-of-a-Kind Family.*
Thayer, Ernest L. *Casey at the Bat: A Ballad of the*
    Republic Sung in the Year 1888.

Humor, K–3

Ahlberg, Janet and Allan. *Funnybones.*
Atwater, Richard. *Mr. Popper's Penguins.*
Allard, Harry. *Miss Nelson Is Missing.*
Burningham, John. *Mr. Gumpy's Outing.*
Cleary, Beverly. *Beezus and Ramona.*
———. *Ramona the Brave.*
Lindgren, Barbro. *The Wild Baby.*
Marshall, James. *Mary Alice, Operator Number Nine.*
Parish, Peggy. *Amelia Bedelia.*
Rey, H. A. *Curious George.*
Scieszka, Jon. *The True Story of the Three Little Pigs.*
Suess, Dr. *And to Think That I Saw It on Mulberry*
    Street.
Viorst, Judith. *Alexander and the Terrible, Horrible,*
    No Good, Very Bad Day.
———. *My Mama Says There Aren't Any Zombies,*
    Ghosts, Vampires, Creatures, Demons, Monsters,
    Fiends, Goblins, or Things.
Ziefert, Harriet. *I Won't Go to Bed!*

Humor, 4–6

Byars, Betsy. *The Pinballs.*
Cleary, Beverly. *Ramona Forever.*
Conford, Ellen. *Lenny Kandell, Smart Aleck.*
Gilson, Jamie. *Do Bananas Chew Gum?*
Gwynne, Fred. *A Chocolate Moose for Dinner.*
Lindgren, Astrid. *Pippi Longstocking.*
Manes, Stephen. *Chicken Trek: The Third Strange Thing that Happened to Oscar Noodleman.*
McCloskey, Robert. *Homer Price.*
Park, Barbara. *Skinnybones.*
Rockwell, Thomas. *How to Eat Fried Worms.*

Mystery, K–3

Adler, David A. *My Dog and the Birthday Mystery.*
Clifford, Eth. *Help! I'm a Prisoner in the Library.*
Cole, Bruce. *The Pumpkinville Mystery.*
Kellogg, Steven. *The Mysterious Tadpole.*
Levy, Elizabeth. *Frankenstein Moved in on the 4th Floor.*
Massie, Diane R. *Chameleon Was a Spy.*
Sharmat, Marjorie W. *Nate the Great.*
Willis, Val. *Secret in the Matchbox.*

Mystery, 4–6

Burnett, Frances Hodgson. *The Secret Garden.*
Fitzhugh, Louise. *Harriet the Spy.*
Howe, Deborah and James. *Bunnicula: A Rabbit-tale of Mystery.*
Konigsburg, E. L. *From the Mixed-Up Files of Mrs. Basil E. Frankweiler.*
Naylor, Phyllis Reynolds. *The Bodies in the Besseldorf Hotel.*

Newman, Robert. *The Case of the Baker Street Irregular.*
Roberts, Willo D. *The View from the Cherry Tree.*
Simon, Seymour. *Einstein Anderson, Science Sleuth.*
Sobol, Donald J. *Encyclopedia Brown, Boy Detective.*
Titus, Eve. *Basil of Baker Street.*

Nature, K–3

Clifton, Lucille. *The Boy Who Didn't Believe in Spring.*
Hopkins, Lee Bennett (ed.). *Moments: Poems about the Seasons.*
Johnston, Tony. *Yonder.*
McCloskey, Robert. *Blueberries for Sal.*
———. *One Morning in Maine.*
———. *Time of Wonder.*
McLerran, Alice. *The Mountain that Loved a Bird.*
Peet, Bill. *Gnats of Knotty Pine.*
———. *Wump World.*
Peters, Lisa. *The Sun, the Wind, and the Rain.*
Ryder, Joanne. *Chipmunk Song.*
Seuss, Dr. *The Lorax.*

Nature, 4–6

Bowden, Joan C. *Why the Tides Ebb and Flow.*
Brittain, Bill. *Dr. Dredd's Wagon of Wonders.*
Callen, Larry. *Night of the Twisters.*
Davis, Hubert. *A January Fog Will Freeze a Hog and Other Weather Folklore.*
Ebensen, Barbara J. *Cold Stars and Fireflies: Poems of the Four Seasons.*
Fleming, Susan. *Trapped on the Golden Flyer.*
George, Jean Craighead. *Julie of the Wolves.*
Giff, Patricia. *The Winter Worm Business.*
O'Dell, Scott. *Black Pearl.*
Ruckman, Joy. *Night of the Twisters.*

Poetry, K-3

Baylor, Byrd. *Amigo.*
Calmenson, Stephanie. *Never Take a Pig to Lunch: And Other Funny Poems about Animals.*
Cole, William. *I'm Mad at You.*
deRegniers, Beatrice Schenk et al. (eds.). *Sing a Song of Popcorn: Every Child's Book of Poems.*
Livingston, Myra Cohn. *Higgledy-Piggledy: Verses & Pictures.*
———. *A Song I Sang to You: A Selection of Poems.*
Merriam, Eve. *You Be Good & I'll Be Night: Jumping-on-the-Bed Poems.*
Milne, A. A. *When We Were Very Young.*
———. *Now We Are Six.*
O'Neill, Mary L. *Hailstones and Halibut Bones.*
Prelutsky, Jack. *My Parents Think I'm Sleeping.*
———. *The Baby Uggs Are Hatching.*

Poetry, 4-6

Adoff, Arnold. *Eats.*
Agree, Rose H. (ed.). *How to Eat a Poem and Other Morsels: Food Poems for Children.*
Cole, William (ed.). *Beastly Boys and Ghastly Girls.*
———. *Poem Stew.*
Dunning, Stephen, et al. (eds.). *Reflections on a Gift of Watermelon Pickle...and Other Modern Verse.*
Fleischman, Paul. *Joyful Noise: Poems for Two Voices.*
Hopkins, Lee Bennett (ed.). *Dinosaurs.*
Hughes, Langston. *Don't You Turn Back.*
Kennedy, X. J. and Dorothy Kennedy (eds.). *Knock at a Star: A Child's Introduction to Poetry.*
Mizumura, Kazue. *Flower Moon Snow: A Book of Haiku.*

Ness, Evaline (ed.). *Amelia Mixed the Mustard and Other Poems.*
Sandburg, Carl. *Rainbows Are Made.*
Viorst, Judith. *If I Were in Charge of the World and Other Worries: Poems for Children and Their Parents.*

Realistic (Problem), K–3

Andersen, Hans Christian. *The Ugly Duckling.* (self-esteem)
Estes, Eleanor. *The Hundred Dresses.* (prejudice)
Keats, Ezra Jack. *Peter's Chair.* (sibling rivalry)
Leaf, Munro. *The Story of Ferdinand.* (peace)
Lionni, Leo. *Fish Is Fish.* (self-concept)
Mathis, Sharon Bell. *The Hundred Penny Box.* (grandparents; memories)
Ness, Evaline. *Sam, Bangs, and Moonshine.* (fantasy vs. reality)
Piper, Watty. *The Little Engine that Could.* (determination)
Rabe, Bernice. *Balancing Girl.* (disability)
Seuss, Dr. *Horton Hatches the Egg.* (commitment)
Viorst, Judith. *The Tenth Good Thing about Barney.* (death)
Zolotow, Charlotte. *The Quarreling Book.*

Realistic (Problem), 4–6

Bauer, Marion. *On My Honor.* (death)
Blue, Rose. *Grandma Didn't Wave Back.* (aging)
Byars, Betsy. *Cracker Jackson.* (wife abuse)
———. *The Not-Just-Anybody Family.* (family)
Cleary, Beverly. *Dear Mr. Henshaw.* (divorce; moving)
Merrill, Jean. *The Pushcart War.* (progress)
Park, Barbara. *Don't Make Me Smile.* (divorce)

Paterson, Katherine. *Bridge to Terabithia.* *(friend-ship; death)*

———. *The Great Gilly Hopkins.* (foster child)

Sachs, Marilyn. *Bear's House.* (family)

Taylor, Mildred D. *Roll of Thunder, Hear My Cry.* (prejudice)

Uchida, Yoshiko. *Journey Home.* (war)

Chapter Seven

Reading instructions, graphs, maps, and tables

Children have more need of
models than critics.
—Joseph Joubert

Sometimes a child may have trouble with schoolwork, not because he doesn't understand or is a slow learner but because he doesn't pay close enough attention to instructions. This is especially true in math and science. Any set of directions must be listened to or read carefully, and a child has to realize that it can cause problems if he's careless or jumps to conclusions. Especially when the instructions are spoken, it's important to make sure they are understood before answering a question or doing a task. Of course, a child can read instructions more than once, but it's best for him to develop the habit of carefully reading what he's being asked before reacting.

Your child will be following directions throughout his life. That's why he must acquire an early appreciation of the need for care and accuracy in dealing with directions. In the next few pages you'll find a series of simple exercises designed to help young children practice paying attention to and following both spoken and written instructions. The skills needed in these first drills can be applied to the later sections of this chapter involving graphs, maps and tables.

Following spoken directions

If yours is a very young child whose reading and writing skills are not very advanced, he can begin to practice complying with spoken directions. Start with simple, one-step procedures requiring the child to react to just one direction before moving to the next exercise. There's no limit to the tasks you could assign. Here are some examples:

- Clap your hands twice.
- Raise your right hand above your head.
- Turn around in a circle.
- Hold up three fingers on your left hand.

Once your child understands the importance of listening to each direction before acting on it, you can go on to two-step instructions. Here again, you should stress that it's critical to listen carefully to the entire set of directions before acting. You can combine the previous instructions, or add new ones:

- Clap your hands once, then tap your right foot once.
- Raise your right hand over your head, then point to the floor with your left hand.
- Draw a circle in the air with your right hand, then hold up three fingers on your left hand.

You can proceed to instructions that include three or four steps as long as the responses required are fairly simple. You may want to have several children participate in these activities by turning them into the "Mother, May I?" game. Before doing the tasks, the child asks, "Mother, May I?" "Yes, you may." Upon successful completion of the tasks, the child advances on a course or receives a point on a score sheet.

- Clap your hands, tap your right foot, and then tap the top of the table with your left hand. ("Mother, may I?")
- Stand up, turn around twice and bring me a paper.
- Pick up your toy, put it on the shelf, then shake my hand.

How can I make a connection in my child's mind between following verbal directions and reading and writing?

It's also a useful to give verbal instructions that require your child to write or draw on paper. You can offer directions in which the first step leads to the second, and so on. The following are examples of three-step instructions.

Provide paper and brown, red, and yellow crayons.

- Draw an ice cream cone on the left side of the page, a balloon in the center of the page, and a banana on the right side of the page. (Wait for the child to complete all of this before continuing.)

- Color the ice cream brown, the balloon red and the banana yellow.

- Write your name in the top right corner of the page, put the date under your name, and then hold up the paper for everyone to see.

These exercises are set up in such a way that the amount of information in the instructions increases, so that your child has to listen carefully and retain the information before acting.

Following written directions

As was true for following spoken instructions, it's a good idea to start very young children with written ones that involve only one step before moving to more complicated exercises. The difference here is that a child must be advanced enough in reading to be able to understand and comply with written instructions. It's best to begin with examples that pose simple tasks.

Instructions such as those given below can be written on cards or on the top of the paper on which the answers will be written. For the sake of variety, you may include exercises calling for physical acts. You may also use the example directions given in the section on following spoken instructions, but keep in mind the limits of your child's vocabulary and reading skills. Here are a few samples using simple words:

- Tap your foot three times.
- Draw two circles and one box.
- Write your name with a red crayon and circle it in yellow.

Second graders usually are able to handle written instructions involving three steps. Most of the examples below have three steps; they can be adapted to two- or four-step drills as needed. For those exercises requiring the drawing of various shapes, you may want to review how a circle, square, and triangle are shaped. Be sure to stress that only by reading the directions carefully and completely will the child be able to plan the placement of the various shapes on the page. These exercises require only paper and red, yellow, and blue crayons. The illustrations are for your information; your child should see only the written instructions.

- Draw a yellow triangle. Draw a red circle to the right of the yellow triangle. Then put a blue square to the right of the circle.

- Draw a blue circle. Put a red triangle inside the circle. Draw a yellow square to the right of the circle.

- Draw a red square. Put a yellow circle around the square. Make a blue triangle inside the square.

You can come up with other exercises that require your child to deal with words or to write answers. For these, only pencil and paper are needed.

- Look at each group of words given below. Which word in each group is different from the others? Draw a line under the one that is different.

  kitten kitten kittens kitten

  house horse house house

  run run ran run

  play ply play play

- Look at the words in each group. Draw a line

under the words that go with the first word. Put two lines under the word that does not go with the first word.

baseball <u>bat</u> <u>game</u> <u>bark</u> (example)

lake water grass boat

house door window sky

school book desk boat

- Write your name on your paper. Write your age under your name. Draw a big circle around your age and name.

It's possible to create other activities that fit the needs and abilities of your own child. An older child can be given more challenging projects that require him to find pictures or information in magazines or newspapers and to act on them.

For example:

- Look at the front page of the newspaper. Find two different stories and read the headline and the first few lines of each one. Write the key word or words that tell what the story is about.

Your goal in all of these exercises should be to offer a clear set of directions, giving the child practice in reading instructions carefully before trying to follow them.

Graphs, maps and tables

Working with graphs
A graph is a kind of diagram used to represent information in a clear, concise form. Graphs are especially useful in simplifying large amounts of information or in displaying how two or more things are connected or related. Because graphs do both of these things

well, they are used quite often even though they don't always give details as completely as tables do.

There are four basic kinds of graphs: bar, line, circle, and picture. Often one kind will be better suited than the others to displaying a particular kind of fact. This will become more obvious as we discuss the types of graphs in more detail.

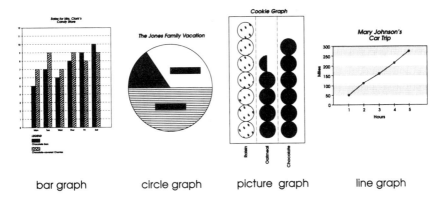

bar graph   circle graph   picture graph   line graph

➡ **Bar graphs.** In a bar graph, amounts are compared by using heavy lines ("bars") which are drawn to scale; that is, in proportion to each other. For example, if amount A is five times greater than amount B, the bar that stands for A will be five times longer than the bar for B.

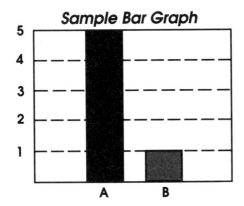

Sample Bar Graph

Bar graphs are generally used to compare two or more sets of amounts.

Your child will be better able to understand why bar graphs are made and how to understand them if you help him make his own bar graphs. Here are the steps involved; some examples follow.

How to make a bar graph

(1) Decide what type of information you want represented on the graph. At first, it's a good idea to choose familiar items that can be easily counted and which have some meaning to your child. For example, you could use a bar graph to show how many chairs, lamps, tables, and beds there are in your home.

(2) Figure out a scale, depending on the space available. Decide how much space you want the largest bar to occupy, and then make the other bars proportionally smaller. If very large numbers are represented on the page, a very small part of the page can stand for a large amount (one inch may represent a thousand miles, for example).

(3) Find the actual length of each bar, based on the scale you've set up. Draw the bars carefully, to make sure each is the right length. The graph should be labelled clearly to show what is represented.

Bars can be laid out vertically (up and down) or horizontally (across), and background lines can be included if they make the graph clearer.

We'll set up a bar graph based on the information in this example:

The children in Mrs. Jones' third-grade class have the following pets:

9 cats	5 mice
10 dogs	3 birds

Set up a bar graph with this information.

(1)   The scale used here will be one animal equals ½ inch. That means the longest bar will be five inches long (since 10 dogs x ½ inch = 5 inches).

(2)   Find the length of each bar, according to the same scale: 10 dogs = 5 inches, 9 cats = 4 ½ inches, 5 mice = 2 ½ inches, and 3 birds = 1 ½ inches.

(3)   Draw a solid line across the paper, near the middle of the page. This will serve as a reference point (that is, zero). Lightly draw lines parallel to this one, ½ inch apart. Draw at least ten of these (to represent ten half-inches), and number these from the bottom to the top, along the left side of the page.

(4)   Make vertical bars to represent each of the four kinds of pets. You can make the bars as thick or thin as you want.

(5)   Under each bar, label the kind of animal it represents. Or you may label the animals in a legend (see example).

(6)   Give the graph a title that explains it, such as "Pets Owned by Children in Mrs. Jones' Class."

The finished graph should look something like the graph on the next page.

Pets Owned by Children in Mrs. Jones' Class

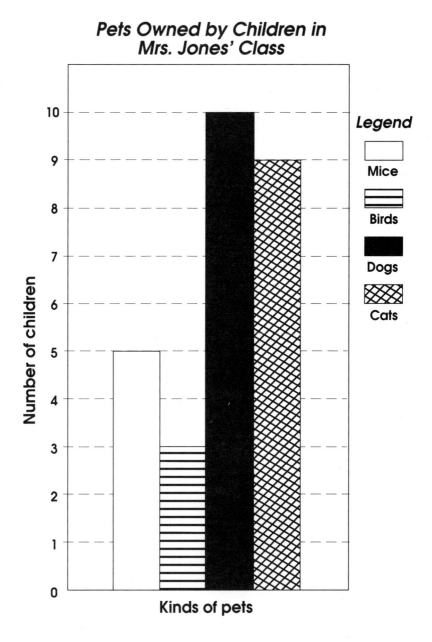

Once you make the basic graph, you have some choices as to how you finish the picture. Your child can color in the graph or leave it blank. The background lines are also optional, but they help make it clear how many items (in our example, pets) are represented. Without the background lines we can see that there are more dogs than cats, mice, or birds, but it's harder to tell how many of each there are.

The rest of the examples are offered so that your child can practice reading graphs and answering questions based on them.

Birds on Mr. McDonald's Farm

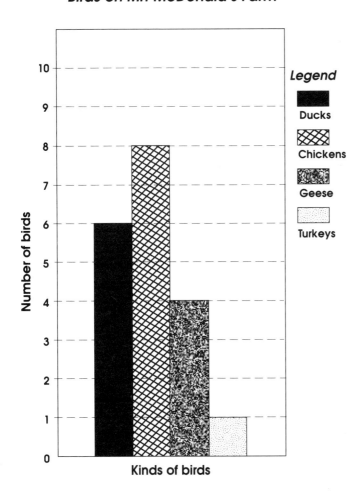

• **Birds on a farm.** Be sure your child looks at the title of the graph and carefully reads the information along the left side and the bottom. After studying this graph, he should be able to answer these questions:

(1) How many turkeys are on the farm?

(2) How many chickens are there?

(3) How many different kinds of birds are there?

(4) There are more of what two kinds of birds?

(5) Altogether, how many birds are on the farm?

In answering the first question, the child should read the legend for the graph until he finds the bar labelled "Turkeys" and then look at the numbers on the left to see how many there are (only one in this case). To answer the second question, he should find the column labelled "Chickens" and then follow the bar up as far as it goes; the numbers on the left show there are eight chickens. For the third question, it is necessary to only count the number of birds listed (four).

In question four, the fact that ducks and chickens are represented by the longest bars tells that there are more of these than the other kinds of birds. The last question requires the child first to find out how many of each kind of bird there are (six, eight, four and one) and then add them together for a total of 19 birds.

• **Life expectancy of different animals.** This graph showing the average life span of five kinds of animals uses horizontal bars. The kinds of animals are listed on the left, and the average number of years each animal lives is shown below. Keeping these points in mind, your child should be able to answer the questions that follow. Although the graph is divided into five-year units, the short lines at the bottom that represent single years should help your child figure out exactly how long each animal lives.

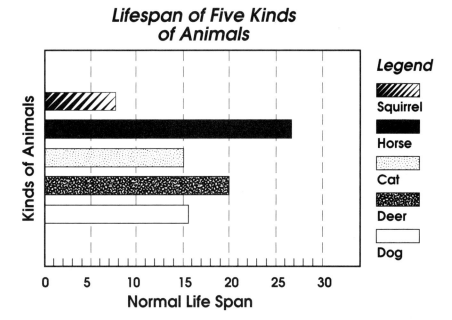

Lifespan of Five Kinds of Animals

Kinds of Animals

Normal Life Span

Legend
Squirrel
Horse
Cat
Deer
Dog

(1) Which animal lives 15 years? (Cat)

(2) Which animal lives the longest? (Horse)

(3) Which animals live longer than the dog? (The horse and the deer live longer.)

(4) How long does the smallest animal live? (The squirrel lives about eight years.)

(5) Which live longer, large animals or small ones? (Large ones live longer than small ones.)

• *Distance of planets from sun.* In the graph below, you can see how far each of the planets in our solar system is from the sun. Each number represents millions of miles, so each amount would be followed by six zeros (for example 250 million = 250,000,000). After your child studies the graph, ask the questions that follow. Obviously, when dealing with such enormous numbers it's not possible to represent exact amounts accurately on a bar graph. However, the graph does get across the idea of how many times farther away from the sun is Pluto than Earth, Venus, or Mercury. Simply giving a young child the exact numbers would not be as meaningful as showing how the distances relate to each other.

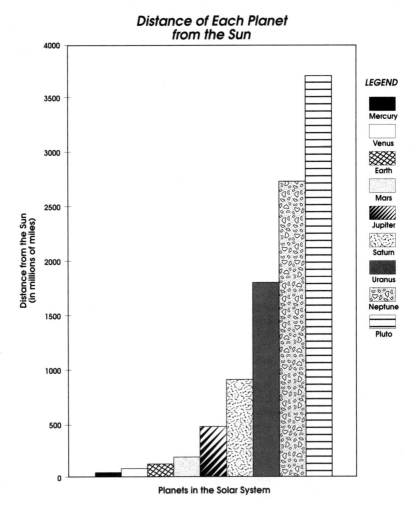

Distance of Each Planet from the Sun

(1)   Which planet is nearly 500 million miles away from the sun? (Jupiter)

(2)   How many planets are more than 500 million miles away from the sun, and what are their names? (Four planets are more than 500 million miles away; they are Saturn, Uranus, Neptune and Pluto.)

(3)   Which two planets are farthest from the sun? (Pluto is farthest away, followed by Neptune.)

(4)   Which planet is closest to the sun? (Mercury)

➡ **Double bar graphs.** Even greater comparisons can be made if the bars are drawn in pairs, with each of the two representing a different thing. Tell your child to look at the following graph and to answer the questions about one week's worth of sales of chocolate-covered cherries and chocolate bars. The key, or "legend," explains which bar represents which kind of candy.

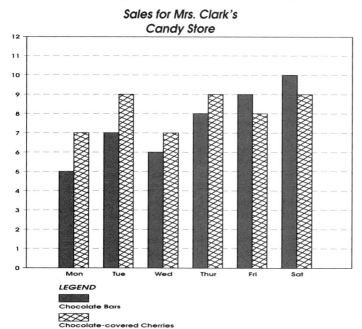

Sales for Mrs. Clark's Candy Store

LEGEND
Chocolate Bars
Chocolate-covered Cherries

(1)   What was the total number of chocolate bars sold on Tuesday, Wednesday, and Thursday put together? (21)

(2)   How many boxes of cherries were sold on Thursday, Friday, and Saturday combined? (26)

(3)   On which days were the most boxes of cherries sold? (Nine boxes were sold on Tuesday, Thursday, and again on Saturday.)

(4)   What was the total number of boxes of candy sold over the whole week, counting both kinds of candy together? (94)

➡ **Triple bar graphs.** Next is a triple bar graph, which compares amounts of three different things. Once again there is a key showing what the different bars represent. Tell your child to study the graph; then ask him the questions that follow it.

Students in Adams Township School

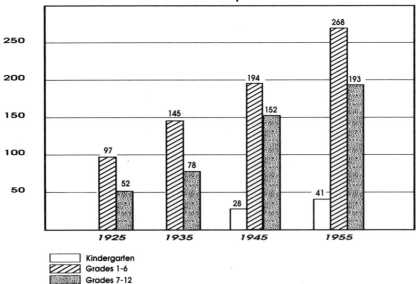

(1)   Did the total number of children in the school get bigger or smaller every ten years? (Bigger)

(2)   In each of the years on the graph, were there more students in grades one through six or in grades seven through twelve? (One through six)

(3)   In what year did the number of students in grades one through six go above 100? (1935)

(4)   Were there more students in the first through sixth grades in 1935 or in 1945? (1945)

➡   **Line graphs.** Line graphs (also called broken-line graphs) are used to show how changes in one variable relate to one or more other variables. Usually one of the variables, such as time or distance, is continuous. We can use this kind of graph, for example, to show how the amount of power used in a city changes over the course of a day.

To set up a broken-line graph for this situation, we have to come up with a scale. As with the bar graphs, one variable is laid out horizontally and the other is presented vertically. Time is normally placed horizontally along the bottom of the graph. Once the scales have been drawn and labelled, points can be put on the graph to represent the given facts. The points are then joined, creating the line. It's possible for the resulting line to be straight, but most often it has a jagged appearance. That's why it's called a "broken-line graph."

•   ***School absences.*** Go over the next graph with your child and ask the questions that come after it. Mrs. Chang kept a record of the absences in her second-grade class during one week. She put the numbers into a graph, with the vertical blocks showing the number of children who were absent and the horizontal lines representing the days of the week.

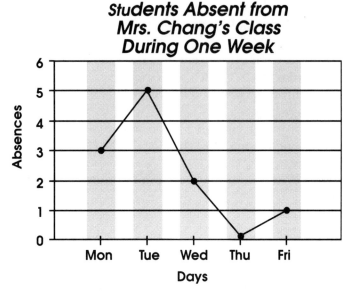

**Students Absent from
Mrs. Chang's Class
During One Week**

(1)   On which two days were the most children absent from class? (Monday and Tuesday)

(2)   On what day were there no absences? (Thursday)

(3)   What was the largest number of absences in one day, and on which day was it? (Five, on Tuesday)

(4)   Were there more students absent on Monday or Wednesday? (Monday)

(5)   Did more of the absent children return to school on Wednesday or Thursday? (Wednesday)

• **Temperature change.** Here's a more complex line graph that represents changes in temperature over a 12-hour period. The outdoor temperature was checked every two hours between six a.m. and six p.m. The numbers were put on a grid on which each horizontal line represents an increase of five degrees, starting at the bottom with 30 degrees. Two-hour periods are labelled across the bottom of the graph. Study the graph and answer the questions.

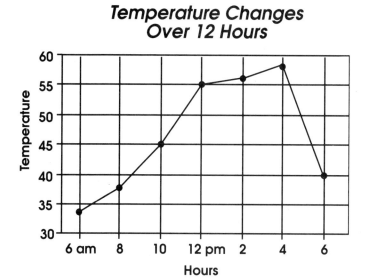

Temperature Changes Over 12 Hours

(1) What was the temperature at noon? (55 degrees)

(2) During the morning, did the temperature go up or down? (Up)

(3) By how many degrees did the temperature change between 8 and 10 a.m.? (It increased 7 degrees.)

(4) What were the highest and lowest temperatures? (The highest was 58 at 4 p.m.; the lowest was 34 at 6 a.m.)

(5) During which two-hour period did the temperature change the most? (The temperature fell 18 degrees between 4 and 6 p.m.)

➡ **Circle graphs.** The circle graph (often called a "pie chart") is a convenient way of showing how parts of something make up the whole (or how the "slices" fit together to make the "pie").

In learning how to tell time, children usually become familiar with a clock face and can understand the division of a circle into halves, thirds, fourths, sixths and even twelfths. In fact, working with circle graphs can help them understand how clocks divide the day into parts: hours, half-hours, minutes, and so on.

A good way to make a child familiar with circle graphs is to make circular cutouts and fold them. Fold the cutout over once to show what a half-circle looks like; fold it again to show a quarter-circle, and once more to make an eighth. This will help your child learn not only circle graphs but also fractions, just as understanding fractions will aid the understanding of circle graphs.

Several circle graphs are included in this section to show both simple and more complicated relationships between parts of things and the whole.

• *Mrs. Smith's flower garden.* Mrs. Smith planted a flower garden, represented by the circle below. Each section of the circle stands for a different kind of flower that she planted. After studying the graph, answer the following questions.

(1) How many different kinds of flowers did Mrs. Smith plant? (Four)

(2) Did she plant more of any one kind than the others? (No)

(3) How much of the garden is taken up by roses and marigolds put together? (Half)

(4) If Mrs. Smith picks half the daisies, how much of the garden will be left with no flowers blooming? (One-eighth)

(5) Altogether, Mrs. Smith paid two dollars for all the seeds in her garden. If each kind of seed costs the same amount, how much did she pay for the aster seeds? (Fifty cents)

Mrs. Smith's Flower Garden

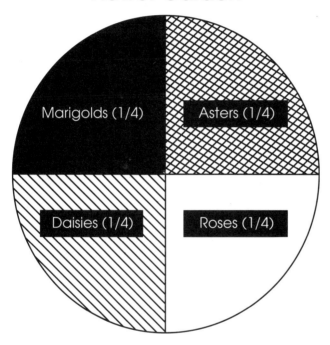

• **Mrs. Smith's vegetable garden.** Mrs. Smith planted a vegetable garden, divided as shown in the circle graph below.

(1) How many different kinds of vegetables did Mrs. Smith plant? (Three)

(2) How much of the garden is planted in corn? (Half)

(3) How much is planted in carrots? (One-fourth)

(4) Is there more corn or lettuce? (Corn takes up half the garden; lettuce only fills one-quarter.)

(5) How much of the garden is taken up by corn and carrots put together? (Three-fourths)

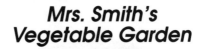

Mrs. Smith's Vegetable Garden

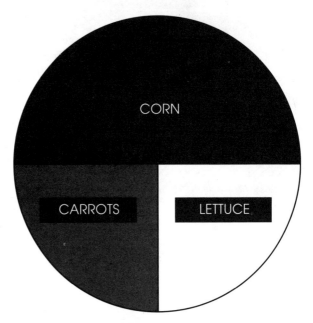

• **Favorite sports.** Each of twelve friends who belong to a neighborhood boys' club named the sport that he liked best. Three sports were most popular; these are shown in the circle graph below.

(1) How much of the graph stands for baseball? (Half) How many of the boys like baseball best? (Six)

(2) One third of the graph stands for the number

of boys who like football best. Football is the favorite sport of how many of the boys? (Four)

(3)   How much of the graph is left to show the boys that like basketball? (The answer is one-sixth: half of the graph, or three-sixths, stands for the number of boys who like baseball, and one-third or two sixths like football. That leaves one-sixth.) How many boys like basketball the best? (Two)

(4)   How much of the graph stands for the number of boys who like baseball and those who like basketball, put together? (Two-thirds or four-sixths) How many boys is that? (Eight)

Favorite Sports of Members of the Boys' Club

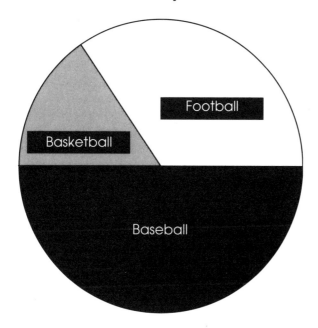

• *The Jones family vacation.* The Jones family spent a 12-day vacation travelling by car, visiting friends along the way and sightseeing in New York. This circle graph shows how the 12 days were spent.

The Jones Family Vacation

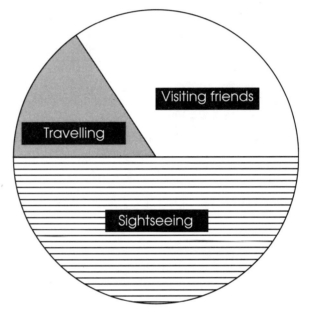

1) One-sixth of the time was spent travelling. How many days is that? (Two)

(2) How many days were spent sightseeing? (Six)

(3) How much of the graph shows the amount of time spent visiting friends? (One-third) How many days is that? (Four)

(4) If the Jones family had spent one more of the 12 days travelling, how much of the graph would show the time the family travelled? (One-fourth, which means three days) If the Joneses still wanted to spend the same amount of time in New York, how much time would be left to visit friends? (Three days)

- ***Buying a cat.*** For his birthday, Ted got a special present from his brother Ben. Ben spent $16 for a pet cat, a cat's bed, and a package of cat food. The graph shows how much of the $16 was spent on each item.

Ted's Birthday

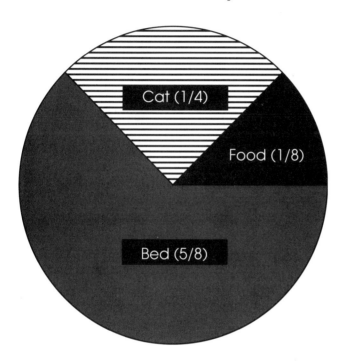

(1)   How much did the cat food cost? ($2)

(2)   How much did the cat's bed cost? ($10)

(3)   How much did it cost to buy a cat to eat the food and sleep in the bed? ($4)

4)   What part of the whole amount was spent on the cat food and bed put together? (Three-fourths, or $12)

➡ **Picture graphs (pictographs or pictograms).** Sometimes, pictures of the things being represented can themselves be used in graphs to show how many of the things there are. When there are not many items being counted, one picture can stand for one thing. In the first bar graph we looked at, for example, a separate picture could be used to represent each animal since there are only ten dogs, nine cats, five mice and three birds owned by the children in the class. If large numbers have to be shown, one picture can stand for dozens, hundreds, or even billions of things. For instance, if we wanted to make a picture graph of how many cars go through a busy intersection in a certain amount of time, there may be so many that one picture of a car may have to stand for a hundred or even a thousand cars. As with any other kind of graph, when a very large number is represented, the amount shown in the picture graph may just round off the actual total.

To understand how to read different kinds of graphs, a child must understand what the word *scale* means. It has different meanings in different kinds of graphs. In a picture graph, *scale* means how many things the picture portrays, while in a map (which is another kind of graph), *scale* refers to how much of the map stands for how much real distance. This is why a road map may say, for example, "one inch equals 50 miles." The first picture graph uses pictures of computer products to represent 10 of each product.

• *Colleen's Computer Store.* Colleen's Computer Store kept track of how many products it sold in one month. The graph shows how many computers, printers, and computer disks were sold during the month. Each picture stands for 10 computers (top row), 10 printers (middle), or 10 computer disks (bottom).

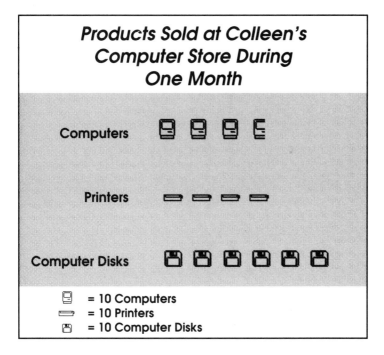

Products Sold at Colleen's Computer Store During One Month

Computers

Printers

Computer Disks

= 10 Computers
= 10 Printers
= 10 Computer Disks

(1)   The store sold the most of which kind of product, and how many of that product were sold? (computer disks—60 were sold.)

(2)   How many printers were sold? (40)

(3)   How many computers were sold? (35; that is, 3 ½ pictures are shown)

• **1990 population for selected countries.** The next graph shows the number of people who lived in Canada, Italy, Japan, the United Kingdom, and the United States in 1990. Each stick figure stands for 25 million people (25,000,000). Because the numbers are so big, they've been rounded off to the nearest million. With this kind of graph we can see which countries have about the same number of people living in them, which have the most, and which have the least. The graph also gets across the idea of millions of people better than just giving the numbers does.

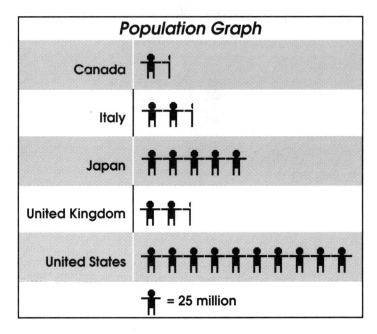

Population Graph

Canada	
Italy	
Japan	
United Kingdom	
United States	

= 25 million

(1)   Which of these countries had the most people? (USA)

(2)   Since there are ten whole stick figures to stand for the number of the people in the United States, about how many people were there in 1990? (250 million)

(3)   Which of these countries had the second most people, and about how many were there? (Japan is second; the almost five stick figures represent close to 125 million people. There were actually 124 million people in Japan in 1990.)

(4)   Which two countries had about the same number of people in them, and about how many were there? (Italy and the United Kingdom each have almost 2 ½ stick figures in their rows, so they each had between 55 and 60 million people in 1990. Italy really had 58

million and the United Kingdom had 57 million.)

(5)   Which of the countries shown had the fewest people, and how many people lived there?   (The population of Canada is represented by just over one stick figure, which means that about 25 million people lived there. The real figure in 1990 was 27 million.)

(6)   Think about how the country with the most people living there compares to the one with the least. Which two countries were those, and how many times more people were there in the biggest country than in the smallest?   (There were almost ten times as many people living in the United States as in Canada.)

(7)   How does the number of people in the United States compare to the number in the country with the next largest population? (There were just over twice as many people in the United States as there were in the country with the second largest population, Japan.)

➡   **Maps.** A map is a special kind of graph. It is a picture of an area drawn to a certain scale. We can use a map to show the whole world, a single country, one city block, or even the inside of one house. Maps are of course a lot smaller than what they represent, but the distances between things on the map should be in proportion to the distances they portray. This is what we mean when we say a map has to be drawn "to scale."

Maps don't need to show every single detail, as a photograph would, but only have to include some of the features in an area. A geographical map shows mountains, valleys, rivers, and so on; political maps show the boundaries between states or countries, where cities are, etc.; other maps can show such information as election results, population comparisons, or other facts.

There are many excellent atlases (books of maps) and other books that include maps for young children. If your child is interested in this kind of material, you can check your local library or bookstore to see what's available from major map publishers such as Rand McNally and Co. or C.S. Hammond and Co. These books have many illustrations as well as plenty of information along with the maps; they often include other kinds of graphs and tables.

• ***Jim's neighborhood.*** We'll begin with a drawing that shows a few major landmarks near a country road where Jim lives. In the picture, you can see that the pond is south of Jim's house, the gas station is to the west, and so on.

This is not quite a real map yet because it doesn't show any specific scale. For example, you can't tell how far it is from one landmark to another, and it would be hard to explain to another person what the relationships among the various features are. Later we will show how this simple drawing can be made into a real map.

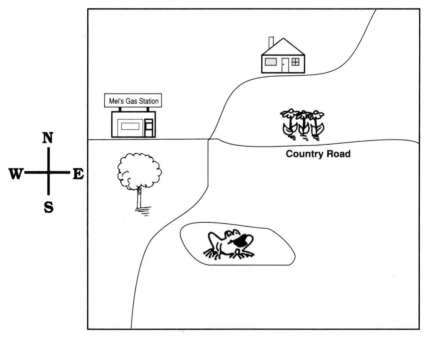

A more accurate way to pinpoint the location of each landmark is to draw a grid of vertical and horizontal lines on the picture. This is a common way of locating specific points on maps. With large maps of the world or of countries, you'll often see (horizontal) latitude and (vertical) longitude lines. On a city map, the streets themselves may form a grid pattern. Sometimes grids are drawn onto maps, with an index to help the map user find a specific place.

- ***Jim's neighborhood with grid.*** The next map has a grid which can be used to find specific points; just read across the bottom until you reach the point you're looking for, and then follow that vertical line up until you get to the horizontal numbered line you need. Here, as in the previous drawing, you are given compass directions. This map also tells that each segment on the grid stands for ¼ mile.

After studying the map, answer these questions:

(1)   Where is Jim's house on the map? (D-3)

(2)   Where is the orchard? (A single tree, with its trunk on B-1, is used to represent all of the trees in the orchard located there.)

(3)   The eastern end of the pond is shown on the map. How could you describe where it is? (A-3)

(4)   While driving on the Country Road, we must turn off to get to Jim's house. This turnoff is near the intersection of which two grid lines? (C and 2)

(5)   Locate the garden and the gas station. (C-3, C-1) How far apart are they? (½ mile)

(6)   How far is it from the gas station to the orchard? (¼ mile)

(7) If Jim walked straight from his house to the edge of the pond marked at A-3, how far would he have to walk? (He'd go ¾ mile, from D-3 to A-3.)

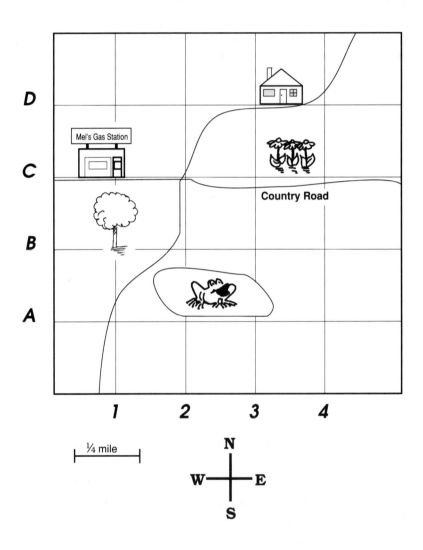

• **City center.** Below is a map showing an area of 20 square blocks in the center of a small city. Here the streets laid out at right angles form a grid. Notice that this map is more abstract than the previous one was. Actual pictures of objects aren't included, only the names and locations of buildings. Study the map. Using the same procedure for locating places by letter and number, answer the questions below.

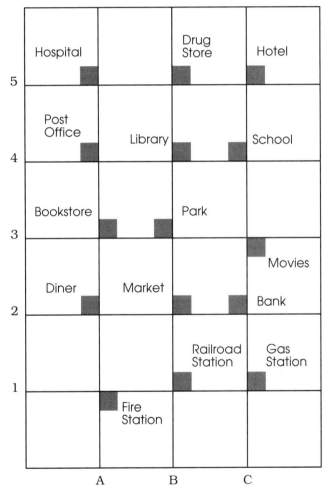

Map of Downtown Somewhereburg

Give the letter and number that shows the location of each building listed below.

(1) Post office: A - _   (9) School: _ - _

(2) Hospital: _ - 5   (10) Hotel: _ - _

(3) Fire station: _ - _   (11) Bank: _ - _

(4) Park: _ - _   (12) Library: _ - _

(5) Railroad station: _ - _   (13) Market: _ - _

(6) Gas station: _ - _   (14) Bookstore: _ - _

(7) Drugstore: _ - _   (15) Movies: _ - _

(8) Diner: _ - _

- **U.S. Map.** Next is a map of the United States. After studying the map, answer the following questions.

1) In which direction must you go to get from Oklahoma to Tennessee? (East)

(2) The borders of California are marked by an ocean, a foreign country, and three states. Name them. (Pacific Ocean, Mexico, Oregon, Nevada, Arizona)

(3) Which three states, other than California, border on Mexico? (Arizona, New Mexico, Texas)

(4) Name the five states in the western and central United States that share a border with Canada. (Washington, Idaho, Montana, North Dakota, Minnesota)

(5) Texas and Florida both border which body of water? (The Gulf of Mexico)

(6) Which state is directly north of Iowa? (Minnesota) Which state is just south of Iowa? (Missouri)

➡ **Tables.** In a table, information is arranged (usually in columns) to show how a set of things relate. By knowing how to read a table, which is a kind of chart, we can find facts quickly, without having to read through a large amount of material.

All tables are labelled in some way, to help the user find the needed information. A table has a title, telling what kind of information can be found in it, and each column has a heading that explains exactly what kinds of facts it contains.

• **Care of house plants.** The following table gives information on taking care of house plants. Study the table and answer the questions given below.

Answer the following questions True or False.

T F (1) Cactus needs soil made of coarse sand and loam.

T F (2) Gloxinia must be kept uniformly moist.

T F (3) African violets should be watered only when the soil is dry.

T F (4) Geraniums should be kept uniformly moist.

T F (5) Potting soil mixture is recommended for Sansevieria.

T F (6) Use a mixture of loam, sand and humus for African Violets.

T F (7) Use potting soil mixture for cactus.

Care of House Plants

Type of Plant	Watering Instruction	Kind of Soil
African Violet	Use Lukewarm water. Keep soil uniformly moist.	Mixture of loam, sand and humus.
Cactus	Wait until soil is dry. Water thoroughly.	Mixture of course sand and garden loam.
Geranium	Wait until soil is dry. Water thoroughly.	Potting soil mixture.
Gloxinia	Soil should be kept uniformly moist.	Open porous soil.
Sansevieria	Water when soil is dry.	Open porous soil.

• **U.S. presidents.** Our final table contains facts about ten of the U.S. presidents. As before, study the information given in each column and answer the questions that follow.

Ten U.S. Presidents

President	Home State*	Age#	Term
George Washington	Virginia	57	1789–1797
John Adams	Massachusetts	61	1797–1801
Thomas Jefferson	Virginia	57	1801–1809
John Quincy Adams	Massachusetts	57	1817–1825
Andrew Jackson	Tennessee	61	1829–1837
Abraham Lincoln	Illinois	52	1861–1865
Theodore Roosevelt	New York	42	1901–1909
Franklin Roosevelt	New York	51	1933–1945
Dwight Eisenhower	New York	62	1953–1961
John F. Kennedy	Massachusetts	43	1961–1963

* This is the state from which each president was elected, not necessarily the state in which he was born.
# This is the age at inauguration.

(1)   Of the ten presidents listed here, which one was the youngest when he took office? (Theodore Roosevelt, who was 42)

(2)   Which president in the group was oldest when he took office, and how old was he? (Dwight Eisenhower, 62)

(3)   Which three presidents were living in Massachusetts when they were elected? (John Adams, John Quincy Adams, John F. Kennedy)

(4)   How many of these presidents were elected during the nineteenth century (the 1800s), and who were they? (Four: Thomas Jefferson, John Quincy Adams, Andrew Jackson and Abraham Lincoln)

(5) Most of these presidents served for two full four-year terms. Which ones served for less than two terms? (John Adams, Abraham Lincoln and John F. Kennedy)

Summary

Your children will be following directions throughout their lives. Helping them learn to follow directions will make learning easier.

You can come up with a wide variety of activities to practice following both spoken and written directions. Use the samples in this chapter as starting exercises.

A good way to practice following directions is to work with graphs, maps, and tables. Ask your child to examine samples in this book and answer questions based on them. There are several kinds of graphs and charts. A little practice will help your child adjust quickly to finding information from each type.

Chapter Eight

Selecting books for children

*A house without books is like a
room without windows.*
—*Horace Mann*

From the time a child first experiences a sense
of independence—by crawling to touch a family pet, for example—he begins to make choices.
All children do. Each one of us thereby begins a lifelong search for the things and the ideas that interest
and please us.

Choice of books

As a parent, you guide your child's choices and actually make some of them when that is appropriate. No
one is surprised that some choices are in your child's
hands, some are in your hands. Look at book selection in that way. During your child's early years, you
probably make most of the choices; later, children
make most of their own selections. But even into
adolescence and adulthood, it is appropriate and
desirable for you to purchase books for your children
and to discuss the ideas and pleasures that are found
in those books. You may think of book-giving either

as a continuing education or as a reminder of the values that reading gives us throughout life.

What this discussion seems to lead to, then, is a parallel series of choices for you and for your child from early childhood to adulthood. With age and experience your child chooses more and more of his own books—but you, too, are always there, choosing books and supporting your child's interests. This changing perspective about the lifelong choice of books may be represented in the diagram below.

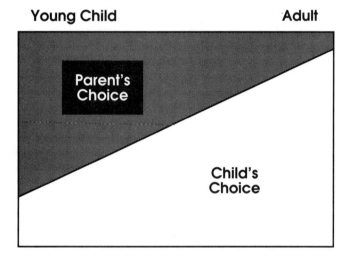

Look for advice

If you want to keep books before your child, you need ideas and resources. You should of course take advantage of the expertise of your local librarian. Ask teachers and other child care people for their advice. They may see interests or needs that you have overlooked. Librarians, teachers, and bookstores often have lists of books that can give you specific titles for typical interests and reading levels. You will also find books with recommended titles and with synopses of the titles listed. We have listed some of these published booklists in Appendix E.

Parents sharing books

One excellent way to demonstrate your interest in books is to share book ideas with your child. If you give your child a book, you might tell her your own reasons for liking the book. And think how impressive it would be if you and your child read the same book and then discussed it. You could each contribute to your mutual knowledge and appreciation of the book.

Book sharing between you and your child should not be a quiz, of course. It is a time for parent and child to look together at the same events and ideas and to discuss them in order to learn together. Some of the most rewarding conversations I had with my son took place when he was twelve or thirteen. He discovered a science fiction book by Frank Herbert called *Dune*. We began reading and talking our way through a trilogy of *Dune* books, wondering how people could live on a desert planet, comparing characters, guessing how the next twist in the plot would turn out. What fun we had together!

All of this happened when my son was becoming an adolescent—a time, according to myth, when he wasn't supposed to talk to his parents but rather was expected to be rejecting parents in the name of freedom. He did some of that, too, but *Dune* gave us a reason to talk to each other, to explore a fascinating world together. We had something more to discuss than our own parent-child relationship. It helps, of course, if that sort of book-sharing relationship begins early in a child's life.

As you search for books for your child, there are a few points to keep in mind. First, long before your child can talk, you can read to him. A very young child will enjoy nursery rhymes and other short, rhythmic pieces, even if he doesn't understand all of the words, because of the tempo and repetitive patterns of the language. Second, you should pick children's books that you like yourself. The pleasure in your voice and the feelings you communicate as you read will affect the way in which your child responds to reading.

Your child's first books should be attractive ones with pictures that relate to the stories. Most young children like drawings that aren't cluttered with too much detail, and those that portray subjects such as the child's favorite activities or animals that are familiar. Cloth-cover books that a child can handle are a good investment, since awkward little hands won't damage them.

There are many excellent references which can guide you in choosing books, especially books for beginning reading students. A number of resources are listed later in Appendix E. One of the best references is *A Parent's Guide to Children's Reading* by Nancy Larrick. You should be able to find this at your library; if not, it's worth the purchase price for parents interested in encouraging children of all ages to read, even children in middle school. The author lists the traits of easy-to-read books:

- The type is large and clear.
- The vocabulary is simple.
- Sentences are short and follow the rhythmic pattern of conversation.
- Printed lines are short, with the line break coming at natural pauses in conversation.
- Pages are uncluttered, and white space is plentiful.
- The pictures give clues that make reading easier and more interesting.

(Nancy Larrick. *A Parent's Guide to Children's Reading.* 5th ed. New York: Bantam, 1982, p. 46)

Although it's obviously not possible to find books that are equally suited to all learners, there are many good suggestions in the lists of books for preschool children given in Appendix A. Here's a quick list of some other books that are especially good for children who are just starting to read:

Recommended Books for Beginning Readers

Author	Title
Leslie Brooke	*Ring O' Roses*
Beatrix Potter	*The Tale of Peter Rabbit*
Ezra Jack Keats	*A Snowy Day*
Aileen Fisher	*In the Middle of the Night*
Robert McCloskey	*Make Way for Ducklings*
Wanda Gag	*Millions of Cats*
Nonny Hogrogian	*One Fine Day*
Marie Hall Ets	*Gilberto and the Wind*

Is this book too difficult for my child?

Once your child begins to read on his own, there are several ways for you to tell if a book is written on a level that he can understand. The first thing to do is to look carefully at the reading books your child is using at school. This will give you an idea of the kind of vocabulary and sentence structure needed for a given age group and grade. If you look at the stories at the end of Chapter 3, you can see stories written for children in early first through late third grade.

Here's a procedure you can follow in deciding if your child can handle a book you've found at your library or bookstore. Have the child read a page of the book to you. Count the number of words on which he hesitates or stumbles, or which he can't make out at all. If only one or two words pose problems, the book matches the child's skills and he can probably handle it with little help from you. If there are three or four words your child doesn't know, the book may still be all right, but you should help him read it the first time. When you find as many as five words that cause problems for a first- or second-grader the book is too hard and will probably frustrate him if he tries to read it on his own. However, if the difficult book is on a subject of high interest to your child, you might want to read it to him, or have him read it along with you. After your child gets to the third grade, you may allow a few more troublesome words per page when he's first reading a book. Should you decide to do this, watch for signs that he's having trouble with entire sentences because he's struggling with many of the individual words.

Books in specific interest areas.

By the time a child gets to the third or fourth grade, he not only gains a certain amount of reading skill; he also develops interest in a variety of subjects. In her book, *A Parent's Guide to Children's Reading,* Nancy Larrick provides the following list of topics of interest to children. The list is included here to suggest subjects you may want to investigate with your child. Titles in these topic areas can be found in the Larrick book. Other possibilities are suggested later in this chapter.

Favorite Books for Boys and Girls

Nursery Rhymes and Picture Books
Easy-to-Read Books
Folk Tales, Fairy Tales, Fables, and Legends
Modern Stories—Real and Fantastic
History—Fact and Fiction
Problems Children Face
Science and Nature
Fun with Magic
Riddles, Jokes, and Nonsense
Poetry for Everyone
Song Books

Another excellent source of information on children's literature is Charlotte S. Huck's *Children's Literature in the Elementary School.* This is a large volume which you may wish to use selectively. Here are seven major kinds of books for children with some examples. These types of books and numerous others are discussed in Huck.

➡ **Picture books**. These are the first books your child encounters, and many examples are given in Appendix A. Some of the favorites in this category are Mother Goose stories and nursery rhymes (all available in a number of versions, with lots of pictures); books about the alphabet (such as Bernice Chardiet's *C is for Circus* or Wanda Gag's *The ABC Bunny*); counting books (including *1, 2, 3 to the Zoo* by Eric Carle and *Count and See* by Tana Hoban); books for helping children understand concepts (for instance, Margaret Wise Brown's *The Important Book* and Miriam Schlein's *Fast is Not a Ladybug* and *Heavy is a Hippopotamus*); wordless picture books (including *The Adventures of Paddy Pork* by John S. Goodall and books by Mercer Mayer such as *A Boy, a Dog, and a Frog*); and of course the large number of books with words and pictures for beginning reading students.

Some popular ones are illustrated versions of *Aesop's Fables* (such as the one adapted by Louis Untermeyer and illustrated by A. and M. Provenson for Golden Press); books by such authors as Margaret Wise Brown (*Home for a Bunny, The Sleepy Lion*); the Brothers Grimm (*Snow White and the Seven Dwarfs*, translated by Randall Jarrell, illustrated by Nancy Burkert for Farrar, Straus); Ezra Jack Keats (*Hi, Cat! and Whistle for Willie*); Leo Lionni (*Alexander and the Wind-up Mouse and Frederick*); and of course, Dr. Seuss (*The Cat in the Hat* and *Horton Hatches the Egg*).

➡ **Traditional literature**. Some of the leading books in this collection are folk tales from different countries, notably those written by Hans Christian Andersen and the Brothers Grimm. Some others are Marcia Brown's telling of the English story *Dick Whittington and His Cat* and the French tale *Stone*

Soup; Paul Galdone's group of English stories including *The Little Red Hen, The Three Bears* and *The Three Little Pigs*; and the well-known stories by Charles Perrault (*Cinderella, Little Red Riding Hood, Puss in Boots* and *The Sleeping Beauty*, for example).

There are a great many versions of the Grimm stories, translated and illustrated by such authors as Wanda Gag and Maurice Sendak. Other types of traditional literature include the fables of Aesop (available in many different versions) and La Fontaine (such as *The Fables of La Fontaine*, adapted and illustrated by Richard Scarry). Many collections of myths and epics are also available, including Roger L. Green's *A Book of Myths, The Myths of the Norsemen, Tales of Ancient Egypt* and *Tales of the Greek Heroes;* Barbara Leonie Picard's *The Iliad of Homer, The Odyssey of Homer Retold,* and *Stories of King Arthur and His Knights;* and Howard Pyle's *The Merry Adventures of Robin Hood.*

➡ **Modern fantasy**. Books of this kind cover a wide range of possibilities, from stories that can be read to (or by) young children, to science fiction for children in upper elementary and middle school. Michael Bond's stories about Paddington Bear (*A Bear Called Paddington* and *More about Paddington*) are especially good for children in the first or second grade, as are Beverly Cleary's *The Mouse and the Motorcycle* and *Runaway Ralph*. Other well-known books of this kind are *Charlie and the Chocolate Factory* and *James and the Giant Peach* by Roald Dahl; *The Wind in the Willows* by Kenneth Grahame; Rudyard Kipling's *Just-So Stories; A Wrinkle in Time* and *A Wind in the Door* by Madeleine L'Engle; Astrid Lindgren's *Pippi Longstocking*; and George Selden's *The Cricket in Times Square.*

➡ **Poetry**. Poetry offers endless possibilities for getting a child interested in what language can do. Whether in the form of simple Mother Goose rhymes or more complex poems for older children, the value of poetry in expanding and developing your child's appreciation of words and his ability to use them is enormous. Younger children enjoy the repetitive words and steady rhythms of the simplest poems. Rhyme can also be an attractive element, but it's not found in all poems. Children like narrative poems very much (in the same way they're interested in finding out "what happens next" in stories) and limericks (the funnier and more ridiculous the better). Children of all ages relish poems with a little humor in them, as well as poems that deal with familiar experiences and animals. Also, children prefer poems using today's language and situations over more traditional poems.

Some of the many collections of children's poetry include: *Poems and Verses about Animals, Poems and Verses about the City,* and *Poems and Verses to Begin On,* all edited by Donald J. Bissett; *The Golden Journey,* a collection of poetry for young people compiled by Louise Bogan and William Jay Smith; *Christmas Bells are Ringing* and *Laughable Limericks,* compiled by Sarah and John E. Brewton; John Ciardi's *I Met a Man* and *You Read to Me, I'll Read to You* (good examples of narrative poems); and the many volumes of poetry compiled by William Cole such as *The Birds and the Beasts Were There, A Book of Animal Poems, Humorous Poetry for Children, Poems for Seasons and Celebrations* and *Story Poems, New and Old.*

➡ **Contemporary realistic fiction.** This group includes books about growing up and living with others, dealing with problems (for instance, physical handicaps, aging and death), living in a society of many racial ethnic and religious backgrounds, and also such topics of interest as animals, humor, sports and mysteries. Some of the most well-known books of this type are the popular stories by Judy Blume (*It's Not the End of the World, Tales of a Fourth Grade Nothing*); Walter Farley (*The Black Stallion*); Louise

Fitzhugh (*Harriet, the Spy*); Marguerite Henry (*Misty of Chincoteague* and *Stormy, Misty's Foal*); Eric Knight (*Lassie Come Home*); and John R. Tunis (*Go, Team, Go!* and *Keystone Kids*).

➡ **Historical fiction**. These books may deal with subjects from prehistoric times, the Old World (Egypt, Rome, Viking adventures), the New World (Indians, colonial times, the frontier, the Civil War), and events and scientific developments of the twentieth century (such as the world wars and space exploration). Some good examples of stories about prehistoric peoples are *One Small Blue Bead* by Byrd Baylor Schweitzer, *Beyond the Gorge of Shadows* by James Harvey, and *And the Waters Prevailed* by D. Moreau Barringer. Stories of ancient times include *Mara, Daughter of the Nile* and *The Golden Goblet* by Eloise McGraw, *I Marched with Hannibal* by Hans Baumann, and *The Dancing Bear* by Peter Dickinson. Tales of Viking deeds are told in Henry Treece's trilogy *Viking's Dawn, The Road to Middlegaard* and *Viking's Sunset*. Children of seven or eight will probably be able to read Clyde R. Bulla's story of medieval adventure, *The Sword in the Tree*. Other stories about this era include *Candle at Dusk* by E. M. Almedignen, *The Door in the Wall* by Marguerite de Angeli, and *One Is One* by Barbara Leonie Picard.

Stories of colonial America include *Thanksgiving Story* by Alice Dalgliesh, *The First Year* by Enid Meadowcroft, and *I Sailed on the Mayflower* by Roger Pilkington. Fortunately, more recent stories about Native Americans no longer portray them as bloodthirsty savages; some of the better children's books about American Indians are *Moccasin Trail* by Eloise McGraw, *Sing Down the Moon* by Scott O'Dell, and *Only the Earth and the Sky Last Forever* by Nathaniel Benchley. There are many books about the American frontier, and these are of great interest to young children. The nine "Little House" books by Laura Ingalls Wilder are very popular, partly because of the television show based on the stories, which can now be viewed in reruns. Others dealing with this period are *Caroline and Her Kettle Named Maud* by Miriam E. Mason, *Bread and Butter Journey* by Anne Colver, and *White Bird* by Clyde Bulla. Many other historical stories about the Civil War and later times can be found.

Remember, whether you're looking for historically based books or titles in any of the other categories, you can check the children's section of your public library. Most library card catalogues are arranged to help you find books about a particular subject.

➡ **Informational books and biography**. Children also enjoy non-fiction books. Here are listed a few examples of these books grouped by topics:

Concept books
- *Shapes and Things* by Tana Hoban
- *A Map Is a Picture* by Barbara Rinkoff
- *How Far Is Far?* by Alvin Tresselt
- *What Makes Me Feel This Way* by Eda LeShan

Informational picture books
- *Charlie Needs a Cloak* by Tomie DePaola
- *Elizabeth Gets Well* by Alfons Weber
- *Clay Sings* by Byrd Baylor
- The series of nine *This Is …* books by Miroslav Sasek (*This Is Australia, This Is Greece, This Is London, This Is New York, This Is Paris*, etc.)

Photographic essays
- *How Kittens Grow* by Millicent Selsam
- *Don't Feel Sorry for Paul* by Bernard Wolf
- *Zaire: A Week in Joseph's World* by Eliot Elisofon

Life-cycle animal books
- *The Mother Owl, The Mother Beaver, The Mother Whale, The Mother Deer*, all by Edith and Clement Hurd

- *Minn of the Mississippi* and *Pagoo* by Holling C. Holling
- *Screamer, Last of the Eastern Panthers* and *Thor, Last of the Sperm Whales* by Robert McClung

Survey books
- *The Doubleday Nature Encyclopedia*, edited by Angela Sheehan
- *The Many Faces of Man* by Sharon S. McKern
- *George Washington's World, Abraham Lincoln's World, The World of Columbus and Sons* and others of the same type by Genevieve Foster.

There are many biographies available for young learners, from simple ones written for beginners to more detailed ones for children in the upper grades. Some of these are:

- *Willie Mays* by George Sullivan
- *Abraham Lincoln, George Washington* and, *Christopher Columbus*, all by Clara Judson
- *The One Bad Thing about Father* (a biography of Theodore Roosevelt told from the point of view of his son Quentin)
- *Me and Willie and Pa, The Story of Abraham Lincoln and His Son Ted*, by F. N. Monjo.

Among the many biographies are those about recent personalities from sports, the arts, and other fields, as well as stories about figures of the more distant past.

Books for different ages

It may seem simplistic to list books for each age of childhood, but the experiences of teachers and librarians indicate that as children's language and experience change, there are books that satisfy those age-related needs. Parents should always be alert, too, to the personal interests of their children. Following are age categories with some examples of books that fit each age.

Books for different ages

Ages 6–7

This age continues an interest in language development and now strives to meet some adult requests for skills. Point of view is very personal, yet they want the good to win and the bad to be punished.

Adkins, Jan. *How a House Happens.*
Ahlberg, Janet and Allan. *Each Peach Pear Plum.*
Aliki. *Feelings.*
———. *Green Grass and White Milk.*
———. *How a Book Is Made.*
———. *A Weed Is a Flower.*
Ardizzone, Edward. *Tim to the Rescue.*
Aruego, Jose. *Look What I Can Do.*
Bishop, Claire Huchet and Kurt Weise. *The Five Chinese Brothers.*
Caines, Jeanette. *Just Us Women.*
Cameron, Ann. *The Stories Julian Tells.*
Cole, Joanna. *The Magic Schoolbus at the Waterworks.*
———. *My Puppy Is Born.*
Conford, Ellen. *Impossible, Possum.*
Cummings, Pat. *Clean Your Room, Harvey Moon.*
Dalgliesh, Alice. *The Bears on Hemlock Mountain.*
Duvoisin, Roger. *Petunia the Silly Goose Stories.*
Flack, Marjorie. *Walter and the Lazy Mouse.*
Freeman, Don. *Dandelion.*
Fuchs, Erich. *Journey to the Moon.*
Gill, Joan. *Hush Jon!*
Ginsburg, Mirra. *Mushroom in the Rain.*
Goble, Paul. *The Gift of the Sacred Dog.*
Golden, Augusta. *Ducks Don't Get Wet.*
Gomi, Taro. *Spring Is Here.*
Gray, Nigel. *A Country Far Away.*
Gross, Theodore Faro. *Everyone Asked about You.*
Guilfoile, Elizabeth. *Nobody Listens to Andrew.*

Havill, Juanita. *Jamaica Find.*

Heide, Florence Parry and Judith Heide Gilliard. *The Day of Ahmed's Secret.*

Hill, Elizabeth Starr. *Evan's Corner.*

Hoban, Tana. *Look Again!*

Hutchins, Pat. *Clocks and More Clocks.*

———. *The Surprise Party.*

Johnson, Angela. *Tell Me a Story, Mama.*

Keats, Ezra Jack. *Whistle for Willie.*

Koren, Edward. *Behind the Wheel.*

Kraus, Robert. *Leo the Late Bloomer.*

Lobel, Arnold. *Frog and Toad Together.*

McCloskey, Robert. *Time of Wonder.*

McFarland, Cynthia. *Cows in the Parlor.*

Peters, Lisa Westberg. *Water's Way.*

Reyher, Rebecca. *My Mother Is the Most Beautiful Woman in the World.*

Rockwell, Anne F. *Olly's Polliwogs.*

Rothman, Joel and Argentina Palacios. *This Can Lick a Lollipop.*

Rylant, Cynthia. *Henry and Mudge and the Bedtime Thumps.*

Scott, Ann Herbert. *Sam.*

Segal, Lore Groszmann. *Tell Me a Mitzi.*

Shaw, Charles. *It Looked Like Spilt Milk.*

Silverstein, Alvin. *Guinea Pigs, All about Them.*

Steig, William. *Amos and Boris.*

Steptoe, John. *Stevie.*

———. *Train Ride.*

Taylor, Mark. *Henry the Explorer.*

Tolstoy, Aleksey Nikolayevich. *The Great Big Enormous Turnip.*

Tresselt, Alvin R. *A Thousand Lights and Fireflies.*

———. *Wake Up, City.*

Turkle, Brinton. *Obadiah the Bold.*

Udry, Janice. *Let's Be Enemies.*

Waters, Kate and Madeline Slovenz-Low. *Lion Dancer.*

Yabuuchi, Masayuki. *Whose Footprints?*

Yashima, Taro. *Crow Boy.*
Yoshida, Toshi. *Young Lions.*
Zemach, Harve. *The Judge.*
Zolotow, Charlotte. *Do You Know What I'll Do?*
————. *Mr. Rabbit and the Lovely Present.*

Ages 8–9

By ages 8 and 9, children have gained considerable independence in reading and they are becoming conscious of others around them. They are more likely to see the viewpoints of others and to like slapstick humor.

Alexander, Sally Hobart. *Mom Can't See Me.*
Ancona, George. *Turtle Watch.*
Arnosky, Jim. *I Was Born in a Tree and Raised by Bees.*
Baylor, Byrd. *The Best Town in the World.*
Beatty, Jerome. *Bob Fulton's Amazing Soda Pop Stretcher.*
Belpre, Pura. *The Rainbow-Colored Horse.*
Bernstein, Margery and Janet Kobrin. *The Summer Maker.*
Blume, Judy. *Tales of a Fourth Grade Nothing.*
Bryan, Ashley. *The Cat's Purr.*
Burch, Robert. *Queenie Peavy.*
Burleigh, Robert. *A Man Named Thoreau.*
Butterworth, Oliver. *The Enormous Egg.*
Dahl, Roald. *James and the Giant Peach.*
De Jong, Meindert. *Far Out the Long Canal.*
————. *Home, Candy.*
Enright, Elizabeth. *Gone-Away Lake.*
Epstein, Sam. *First Book of Codes and Ciphers.*
Epstein, Sam and Beryl. *Jackpot of the Beagle Brigade.*
Fitzhugh, Louise. *Harriet, the Spy.*
Fox, Paula. *How Many Miles to Babylon?*
————. *Maurice's Room.*

Fritz, Jean. *The Cabin Faced West.*

———. *Shh! We're Writing the Constitution.*

Garelick, May. *What Makes a Bird a Bird?*

Gibbons, Gail. *Beacons of Light.*

Giff, Patricia Reilly. *Laura Ingalls Wilder: Growing Up in the Little House.*

Goble, Paul. *Her Seven Brothers.*

Goldsmith, Diane Hoyt. *Pueblo Storyteller.*

Green, Constance C. *The Unmaking of Rabbit.*

Hamilton, Virginia. *Zeely.*

Hicks, Clifford B. *Alvin's Secret Code.*

Howe, James. *Morgan's Zoo.*

Hunter, Edith Fisher. *Child of the Silent Night.*

Key, Alexander. *The Forgotten Door.*

Lexau, Joan M. *Striped Ice Cream.*

Lionni, Leo. *Swimmy.*

Little, Jean. *Take Wing.*

MacLachlan, Patricia. *Seven Kisses in a Row.*

McGovern, Ann. *Runaway Slave: The Story of Harriet Tubman.*

McKee, David. *Mr. Benn; Red Knight.*

Miles, Miska. *Annie and the Old One.*

Murray, Michele. *Nellie Cameron.*

Peare, Catherine Owens. *The Helen Keller Story.*

Ryder, Joanne. *White Bear, Ice Bear.*

Schulz, Charles. *Snoopy and His Sopwith Camel.*

Slobodkin, Florence. *Sarah Somebody.*

Steel, William O. *Winter Danger.*

Stolz, Mary. *The Bully of Barkham Street.*

Turkle, Brinton. *The Fiddler of High Lonesome.*

Walter, Mildred Pitts. *Ty's One-Man Band.*

Warburg, Sandol Stoddard. *Growing Time.*

What Do Animals See, Hear, Smell, and Feel? National Wildlife Federation.

White, E. B. *Charlotte's Web.*

Yolen, Jane. *The Emperor and the Kite.*

Ages 10–12

During this age range, most girls reach pubescence and both sexes become interested in personal identity, body development, relations between the sexes. Family issues and parental control begin to come to mind, as do jobs, hobbies, and the broad world outside their neighborhood.

Armstrong, William. *Sounder.*
Blume, Judy. *Then Again, Maybe I Won't.*
Byars, Betsy. *The Summer of the Swans.*
Carruth, Ella Kaiser. *She Wanted to Read: The Story of Mary McLeod Bethune.*
Christopher, John. *The City of Gold and Lead.*
Clymer, Eleanor Lowenton. *My Brother Stevie.*
Donovan, John. *I'll Get There, It Better Be Worth the Trip.*
Embury, Barbara. *The Dream Is Alive: A Flight of Discovery Aboard the Space Shuttle.*
Engdahl, Sylvia Louise. *Enchantress from the Stars.*
Farmer, Penelope. *The Summer Birds.*
Fox, Paula. *One-Eyed Cat.*
Franchere, Ruth. *Willa: The Story of Willa Cather's Growing Up.*
Frank, Anne. *Anne Frank: The Diary of a Young Girl.*
Freedman, Russell. *The Wright Brothers.*
George, Jean Craighead. *Julie of the Wolves.*
———. *Water Sky.*
Goldreich, Gloria. *What Can She Be? A Lawyer.*
Goor, Ron and Nancy. *Insect Metamorphosis.*
Greenberg, Jan and Sandra Jordan. *The Painter's Eye: Learning to Look at Contemporary American Art.*
Greene, Constance C. *A Girl Called Al.*
Hamilton, Virginia. *The Mystery of Drear House.*
Henry, Marguerite. *Black Gold.*
Hitchcock, Alfred. *Alfred Hitchcock's Daring Detectives.*

Hunt, Irene. *Across Five Aprils.*
Jones, Weyman B. *Edge of Two Worlds.*
Keegan, Marcia. *Pueblo Boy.*
Kidder, Harvey. *Illustrated Chess for Children.*
Kroeber, Theodora. *Ishi, Last of His Tribe.*
L'Engle, Madeleine. *The Moon by Night.*
Lester, Julius. *To Be a Slave.*
Lewis, C. S. *The Voyage of the Dawn Treader.*
Mann, Peggy. *My Dad Lives in a Downtown Hotel.*
McHargue, Georgess. *Funny Bananas: The Mystery in the Museum.*
McKissack, Patricia C. *Mary McLeod Bethune.*
Meltzer, Milton. *Mary McLeod Bethune: Voice of Black Hope.*
Mollel, Tololwa M. *The Orphan Boy.*
Neville, Emily Cheney. *Berries Goodman.*
———. *It's Like This, Cat.*
Nixon, Joan Lowry. *A Family Apart.*
O'Dell, Scott. *Black Star, Bright Dawn.*
Paulsen, Gary. *The River.*
Peck, Robert Newton. *A Day No Pigs Would Die.*
Perl, Lila. *The Great Ancestor Hunt.*
Picard, Barbara Leonie. *One Is One.*
Radowski, Colby. *Sydney, Herself.*
Ravielli, Anthony. *Wonders of the Human Body.*
Robinson, Jackie. *Breakthrough to the Big League.*
Robinson, Veronica. *David in Silence.*
Rodgers, Mary. *Freaky Friday.*
Rodriguez, Consuelo. *Cesar Chavez.*
Ross, Frank Xavier. *Racing Cars and Great Races.*
Siebert, Diane. *Mojave.*
Simon, Seymour. *101 Questions and Answers about Dangerous Animals.*
———. *The Secret Clocks: Time Sense of Living Things.*
Smith, Doris Buchanan. *A Taste of Blackberries.*
Southall, Ivan. *Josh.*
Stanley, Diane and Peter Vennema. *Shaka: King of the Zulus.*

Steele, Mary Q. *Journey Outside.*

Taylor, Mildred. *The Road to Memphis.*

Tunis, John Roberts. *His Enemy, His Friend.*

Uchida, Yoshiko. *The Happiest Ending.*

——. *Journey Home.*

——. *Journey to Topaz.*

Voigt, Cynthia. *Homecoming.*

Walker, Paul Robert. *The Pride of Puerto Rico: The Life of Roberto Clemente.*

Wersba, Barbara. *The Dream Watcher.*

Whitfield, Dr. Philip. *Can the Whales Be Saved? Questions about the Natural World and the Threats to Its Survival.*

Wier, Ester. *The Loner.*

Wojciechowska, Maia. *Shadow of a Bull.*

Yep, Laurence. *The Lost Garden.*

Expanding your child's interests

Tracking your child's reading

You may find it useful to keep track of the books that your child chooses to read. With a little prompting, older children can do this on their own. Younger ones can copy down the names of the books, or write their own names on a title card attached to the books they read. If you want to make a display to put on the refrigerator or in your child's room, make a book caterpillar. Cut out equal circles on which your child can write the titles of books read. Tape each new circle to the previous one and everyone can watch the book caterpillar grow.

What if my child only wants to read one kind of book?

Whatever recording method you set up, it can give you an idea of what kind of reading your child is doing. If the list shows that your child is reading all of one kind of material, you will probably want to introduce some other types. A chart like the one below is helpful in promoting varied reading.

Directions: Write the titles of the books your child reads in the spaces below. Write the identification number for each book inside the pie chart, putting the number into the topic "slice" which best describes the book.

	Author	Title	Date
1.			
2.			
3.			
4.			
5.			
6.			

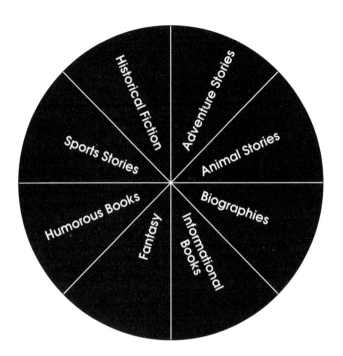

Dealing with a narrow approach to reading
Children often seem to latch on to one kind of book.
For example, they choose only non-fiction books about
rocks and minerals because "I want to learn something when I read." That's fine. You certainly don't
want to argue against an interest in learning, even if
it is a bit narrow. You can point out to older children
that they can learn about human nature from fiction,
though that may be a little abstract for a younger
child. It's usually better to try to expand reading
interests through more subtle means. In dealing with
the child who only wants to read about rocks, you
might point out other non-fiction books with a focus
on plants or animals. Next, you could pick up a
biography about a famous scientist. Perhaps you
could page through the biography and make comments

about events that might interest your child. Maybe she'll pick it up and read more. Science fiction might also be a natural step in the expansion of her reading interests.

Unfortunately, some children may simply refuse to read at all. The very worst thing to do if this happens is to threaten them or force them to read. The best way to address the problem is to help the child succeed, by offering attractive books and by reading together. Ask your child's teacher or librarian for their advice if you have this problem in your home.

High interest books and quick-read books are especially important for a parent dealing with a child who won't read. Many easy-to-read books are now available on a variety of topics; you can find titles on "grown-up" subjects such as space flight, and avoid books that an older child may think are only for "little kids."

Again, the key to helping a child who doesn't like to read is to lead him to success in reading. Children who have problems with reading will continue to need help, even with easy books. You can lend a hand just by taking the time to read with your child.

Resources for learning and reading

As we've suggested throughout these chapters, your local public library is one of the best places to go when you want to help your child advance in reading. To get an idea of the variety of books available for children, talk to the librarian, look through the card catalogue, or just browse the shelves of the children's section. Other useful information can be found in the books listed in Appendix E.

Summary

- Even if your child is too young to read, you can encourage him to become interested in books by reading to him.

- There are many resources to guide parents as they select books. See Appendix E.

- If your child only wants to read one kind of book, try to widen his interests by bringing home books on other subjects.

- Children's interests typically change from age to age; so do their reading levels. An age related book list can help you open new opportunities for your child.

Chapter Nine

Flexibility and reading speed

We learn to do by doing.
—John Dewey

O nce past the basic skills of reading, your child will read all kinds of material for many different purposes—to get information, to enjoy an adventure, to pass a test, and so on! Help your child prepare for this by showing him that he can apply basic reading skills to more complex tasks.

A child in the fourth or fifth grade should understand that he already has many of the skills that he needs to read a variety of books. Across the years he has developed a sense of order and of how things fit together, and an appreciation of how to follow ideas to a conclusion. These skills

Can my child apply the techniques in this book to all subjects in school?

are as useful in reading American history or science as they are in reading the simple stories of the early grades. Most children do not realize that they have developed many reading skills and habits over the years. Sometimes it's helpful to remind them that they have these skills that will help them to read content. They will gradually become better at reading each school subject.

By the time they get to fourth grade, children have seen a great variety of writing forms. Even a first grader has probably been given written instructions for making simple things such as hand puppets or paper cutouts. These directions may have been illustrated to show each step. Pictures help young learners make the connection between spoken and written language. Early reading books also may include questions that help children focus on the text. Illustrations, questions, subheads, and similar techniques are devices that authors use to clarify the text and to make it easier for a reader to follow the ideas. Proficient readers use those devices and also construct some of their own.

Are there special techniques designed to help my child study?

A basic procedure for study-reading

The PARS approach to study-reading

Any job seems easier and more organized if we follow a procedure in doing it. For a younger student who is just beginning to find ways to tackle study-reading, the four-step PARS approach is a useful way of organizing the task. "PARS" means:

- Set a **P**urpose for reading.
- **A**sk questions related to the purpose.
- **R**ead to answer the questions.
- **S**ummarize in your own words what you've learned.

➡ **Purpose**. The first step in the PARS process is to decide why to read something. Most students are likely to say that they're reading because they have to. While this may be an accurate statement about school work, it's not very helpful. A student has to get beyond this view and begin to ask, "What can I get out of reading this assignment?"

At first, your child will probably need help in figuring out his reasons for reading something. One way you can help is by describing your own reasons for choosing to read certain kinds of books. Why do you like those books? If you were the child, how would you expect to benefit from reading the assignment he's about to read? You can be a good role model for finding a purpose for reading. For example, you can show your child how to use chapter headings and subheadings to help focus the purpose. (For more on this particular technique, see next section—"ask".)

When your child is first learning to set a purpose for reading, you should encourage him to talk to himself about what he can see that is interesting or helpful in this article. Although it's best for a young learner to come up with his own reading purpose, you should keep in mind that the child is inexperienced at setting purposes and may need a little guidance at first. Talk to your child about some of the following purposes—when appropriate:

PURPOSES FOR READING IN ENGLISH
Literature

- To understand how others act and feel.
- To understand a way of life other than your own.
- To understand yourself better through the experiences of others.
- To extend your experiences beyond your present situation to other times and places.
- To understand different kinds of written expression, such as poems, short stories and plays.
- To find out how others have solved problems that might be similar to your own.

Writing

- To understand the basic units of written expression, such as sentences and paragraphs.
- To find ways of presenting thoughts and ideas in writing.
- To understand how others have organized and presented their ideas.
- To learn the standards of "correctness" for putting words into written form.

PURPOSES FOR READING IN SOCIAL SCIENCES
History

- To understand how important events happened in the past.
- To understand how people have lived according to where they are in time and place.
- To learn about certain people who have had a large effect on the lives of others.
- To understand how past events have affected our present lives.
- To understand how history is being made today.

Contemporary Cultures

- To understand other societies and how people live in them.
- To compare our own way of life with that of others.
- To realize the problems other societies face.
- To understand how different cultures of the world are connected.

American Society

- To understand different institutions that affect every citizen's life.

- To learn how each of us can take part in public decisions.
- To understand the various subcultures within our society.
- To understand the values of our society.
- To understand the problems faced by the whole nation.

PURPOSES FOR READING SCIENCES
Life Sciences

- To understand how different forms of life are part of an overall system.
- To appreciate the variety of kinds of life.
- To understand the relationships among different forms of life.
- To understand how changes affect the balance of nature.
- To understand man's role in the ecology of the earth.

Physical Sciences

- To understand the basic forces that act upon the world of living things.
- To learn basic laws that can be applied to our experiences.
- To understand how technology affects our lives.
- To go beyond how things appear to a more complete understanding made possible only through science.

PURPOSES FOR READING MATHEMATICS

- To learn mathematical operations.
- To learn how to solve problems.
- To learn how to apply mathematical principles.
- To learn the special "language" of mathematics, such as tables and graphs and the calculator.

➡ **Ask.** The next step involved in the PARS approach is to ask questions. These questions should relate to the purpose your child has set for reading. As she glances ahead at the text, what does she want to learn? What is she curious about? How will she know that she is making satisfactory progress in this text? A good reader is always asking questions. Encourage your child to think of these questions as road signs, telling where she's going and whether she has gotten there. For almost any piece of writing, it's possible to ask about the author's purpose in writing, about the accuracy of the information, the main ideas, conclusions, and the evidence. Here are some sample questions a reader might ask:

- What was the author's purpose for writing this?
- What are the main ideas here?
- What claims is the writer making?
- What evidence is given to back up the author's claims?
- Which facts are most important?
- What does the writer conclude from the facts?
- Do the facts back up what the author is saying?
- From where do these facts come?

One source of questions can be found in subheads. As your child previews a chapter, encourage her to turn some chapter subheadings into questions. Try making questions of these titles:

- *Religion influences medieval thought about the universe*

(Example: How did religion affect the way people

thought about the universe during the Middle Ages?)

- *European history affects certain trends*
- *Internal combustion engines*
- *All machines waste energy*
- *Building a unified paragraph*
- *Arctic exploration*
- *Amphibious animals*

Even with a short heading, it's possible to come up with a whole series of questions to which we can look for answers while reading. In the case of *Amphibious animals*, for instance, some questions might be: What does *amphibious* mean? What makes an animal amphibious? How did amphibious animals develop? Where are they found?

Once your child realizes that headings can carry meaning and can lead to questions about the reading, you can point to illustrations, boldface words, and chapter summaries as other sources to stimulate advance questions.

➥ **Read.** Once he sets a purpose and asks himself questions about what he's about to read, your child is ready to begin reading. He now has a plan for taking in information and ideas. By following the plan, he will be more active and positive than if he had just started reading with no clear direction. Having a structure laid out in advance encourages your child to remember and to build meaning as he goes.

While reading, your child should talk to himself about what he is learning, about the things that are not clear, about ways to answer the questions he raised earlier. Making notes is another way to be an active reader and a way of seeing whether or not questions were answered.

When we read a novel, a letter, a newspaper, or a recipe, we fit the information to our own interests and needs with little or no conscious effort. Study-reading takes a bit more planning. Work with your child until he learns to map out an approach to study-reading. You may even find that the planning leads your young learner to prepare for a reading task with paper, pencil, reference books, and singular concentration.

➤ **Summarize.** Learning becomes fixed in a child's mind when that child is able to put ideas into his own words. This is what we mean by *summarizing*, which is the final step in the PARS process. After completing a well-planned reading task, help your child wrap it all up by saying how the purpose that he set for the reading has been achieved, and how his questions can be answered. He should be able to tell what the main ideas are, what they mean to him, and how he would give someone else a bird's-eye view of what he learned.

The form that reading material takes on in our minds as we read it is the summary. It is helpful for a learner to write a two or three sentence summary as a way to bring the work to a satisfactory conclusion and as a means for recalling the important ideas—perhaps as a review for a test.

P A R S Technique

P: Set a *purpose* for reading. Make it relevant.

A: *Ask* questions about the text that will guide our thinking as you read.

R: *Read* with purpose and questions in mind; that is, with a sense of how you will use the information.

S: *Summarize* in your own words what you have read.

This PARS system of study-reading is simple enough for children in the first years of school, but it can also be applied to any level of reading. Your child will have to practice and will benefit from your guidance, but once he learns the system, he can study independently.

Learning to read more efficiently

There will be times when your child has to read large amounts of material in order to answer a few questions. He may be doing research for a paper, trying to find certain kinds of stories in a newspaper, or answering questions to an open-book test. Your child needs to apply what's known as "efficiency reading" to handle these kinds of tasks.

In efficiency reading, the aim is to read as quickly as possible for a specific purpose. It's based on the idea that we can read something several times faster than usual and still pick up the basic meaning. Some speed-reading programs claim that a person can learn to read as fast as he can turn the page. While this may seem a little hard to believe, high school and college students have been proven able to read from 1000 to 5000 words per minute in certain situations.

Speed-reading

Speed-reading or page-thinking can be helpful for a typical school assignment because it enables a person to read material twice in the same amount of time it would normally take to read it once. The first time through the reading can serve as a sort of preview for the second time. Also, speed-reading allows a student to review a previous assignment quickly just before a class discussion or test.

Speed-reading is a deliberate attempt to read faster by using only enough cues to think about the ideas on a page. The reader forces herself to move faster and faster and asks herself what ideas are developing rather than focusing on saying every word.

Even a child in elementary school can learn to read faster simply by using the index finger as a guide. When practicing, the child can gradually increase how fast the finger leads the eye across the page.

Skimming

Skimming is not the same as speed-reading. In skimming, the goal is usually to pick out specific ideas, whether they be main themes, certain details, or important words. A reader might also skim to find out if a piece of writing fits his purpose or if it's worthwhile to spend time reading more closely. Not only children practice skimming; adults skim when they look over materials to set work priorities, decide on responding to correspondence, browse at the library, and so on.

Whether a person is speed-reading or skimming, the principle is the same: moving faster than normal and understanding what is read at the higher speeds. Once a person can take in what he reads more quickly, he needs to practice reading at an even faster rate. To convert speed-reading into skimming, the reader only needs to keep in mind that he's looking for certain items in the text and not trying to grasp all the important details.

Practicing speed-reading and skimming

You can help your child practice speed-reading and skimming. These techniques can make a difference even if they're practiced for only a few minutes each week. It's easy to tell how fast your child reads. Give him a page or two to read and clock how long it takes in words per minutes. For children in the later grades of elementary school, you should start with passages of no more than 1000 words. However, as the reading speed increases, you can use longer readings. Here's the formula for figuring out reading speed:

$$\frac{\text{words read}}{\text{time (in seconds)}} \times 60 = \text{average words per minute}$$

(Number of words in the passage, divided by the number of seconds it took to read it, times 60 equals reading speed in words per minute.)

Of course, it's most important that your child understands what he is reading. To make sure that he is getting meaning as his reading speed increases, ask him questions about the reading material or have him sum up what he has read. As you keep track of the reading speed, you can also record the "comprehension score" (how many questions about the reading were answered correctly). Use a standard number of questions each time so that the comprehension scores will be comparable to each other. A table like this can be used for tracking progress is increased speed. You can use this table as a way of prompting your child to improve speed and comprehension.

RATE RECORD

Date	Passage Description	Words Per Minute	Comprehension Score
___	_____	_____	_____
___	_____	_____	_____
___	_____	_____	_____
___	_____	_____	_____

Encourage your child to practice skimming by looking for specific bits of information in a passage. Find an article and give your child two or three tasks to finish within a limited time. In an article about the history of manned space flight, for instance, you might say, "Let's see how long it takes you to find the year when the first jet-propelled airplane flew," or "Find the names of as many pioneers of flight as you can, and tell why each one is important." Then let him know how many seconds it took him to report back. This kind of drill will make a game of finding information as quickly as possible. Then your child may ask how he can improve his skimming techniques. Success with these drills will build your child's confidence in his reading ability, and will help him learn how to adjust reading to a purpose.

You and your child can use the following checklist to review the skills needed for efficiency reading.

Efficiency Reading Checklist

	not sure	never	some-times	usually	always
1. I can read fast and understand what I read.	___	___	___	___	___
2. When reading quickly, I look for main ideas.	___	___	___	___	___

3. Before reading, I
   preview to see how fast
   I should read.   ___   ___   ___   ___   ___
4. I change reading speed,
   depending on what I'm
   reading.   ___   ___   ___   ___   ___
5. I skim when looking for
   a single fact or other
   item.   ___   ___   ___   ___   ___
6. When skimming, I try to
   get meaning from
   context.   ___   ___   ___   ___   ___
7. I read silently without
   saying the words.   ___   ___   ___   ___   ___
8. I read groups of words
   rather than one word at
   a time.   ___   ___   ___   ___   ___
9. I do not look back at
   what I've already read. ___   ___   ___   ___   ___
10. I try to keep increasing
    my rapid-reading speed. ___   ___   ___   ___   ___

Summary

- Your child can apply the skills of basic reading in studying other subjects.
- Chapter headings and subheadings can help us form questions about what we intend to read.
- Using the "PARS" study-reading method (purpose-ask-read-summarize) can make a learner's study efforts more effective.
- Speed reading and skimming can help us get more out of reading.

Chapter Ten

How to succeed
with your child

Train a child in the way he should go; and
when he is old he will not depart from it.
—*Proverbs 22:6*

Y ou want your child to succeed as a learner, and
you also want to succeed in helping him to
learn. To establish some perspective, let's examine your role and recap some approaches that may
help you.

Not a classroom teacher

The classroom teacher is primarily responsible for
planning the approach and the materials for
instructing her pupils. She identifies specific
skills and objectives to be worked on. You help
your child by answering his questions and making assignments fit him as an individual. You
try to help him gain self-confidence, to see that

**How am I
different from
a teacher?**

he can learn to read. You give him the opportunity to
practice and indicate that you believe he can learn.

You are not an evaluator in the sense the teacher is.

In the typical classroom, the teacher judges a child for progress and oftentimes for a grade. You encourage progress but have no intention of putting a grade on his performance. In a sense you sit down and ask, "How can we work together to improve your reading?" You then proceed without pressure or threat of failure. If a teacher says your child does not understand the vocabulary, one of your goals will be to discuss the difficult words and help her understand. Part of that help may include searching the library for magazines, newspapers, or books that deal with those words and ideas, but in a simpler manner. Thus, in a non-threatening way you provide a real learning opportunity for your child. (This is not to say the teacher is a threatening, authoritarian figure, but unfortunately the child often sees him as a judge.)

The home environment

Making the learning atmosphere different from the classroom may increase your chances for getting your child to read or to find that reading has value for him. In the classroom there are children who become competitive. The teacher may even encourage a competitive atmosphere. With you, the only competition a child has comes from standards the two of you work out. It's bound to be more relaxed.

What are the differences between the classroom and the home?

When the child performs for the classroom teacher, he has to do so in a limited time in front of other children. A teacher is often concerned with making progress across a number of pages in a book. Consequently, time seems important.

With you, your child is not pressured by time and he performs only for you. You do not have to cover material in a given time. If the child needs explanation or encouragement, you take the time to give it. The classroom teacher is necessarily pressured by the needs and behavior of the other children, but you don't have those pressures. This is not to say you always have control over the atmosphere and the time in which you work. There are restraints on you, too. But you can permit more freedom than the child is likely to find in the classroom. Hopefully, you will be able to create a helpful atmosphere and pace.

No one expects you to have the technical training of a teacher. Your role is more that of an adult friend with a little more training and background than your child. Using this book should also give you some self-assurance.

Remember: even if you have nothing else to offer, you can give encouragement. The fact that you choose to spend two hours or so a week with your child alone is a valuable contribution to a child's ego and motivation to learn. You are saying, "I believe in you." Your major contribution may be that emotional boost. Someone thinks he can learn, and so the child will try his best. That is the attitude you should have and work to develop in the child. In addition, you can contribute solid guidance in learning, assuming you have some knowledge of the skills of reading.

Getting started with home lessons

Visit your child's school and get yourself oriented. Get to know your son or daughter's teacher. Seek out the teacher's advice if you don't know how to get started on your work at home with your child. It would be helpful to visit the school library or public library to see what resources are available to you there.

How should I plan my work with my child?

The counselors and the vice-principal might give you some tips about working with your child.

Preparing home lessons

A general rule to follow with your home lessons is that no single activity should take more that ten to fifteen minutes. You may want to focus on one objective, to develop a particular skill, but make sure you try to achieve it with a variety of activities. He reads to you; you read to him; he writes some questions; together you discuss ways of answering those questions. Naturally, the age and personality of the child will determine how often activities have to be changed.

Have different materials and ideas ready. Outline what you want to try, and decide on the time you want to spend. Gather materials and prepare for more than you think you will need in case your child moves faster than anticipated.

Being prepared, however, does not prevent spontaneous activity if the occasion arises. If your child has something he has read and would like to discuss, fine. One of your primary purposes for being there is to help and encourage. One tutor, for example, was working with a child who wouldn't say more than a mumbled yes or no. The tutor had brought some pictures of prehistoric animals and was asking the child if he knew what they were or that they once lived on earth. The child responded, "No," but the tutor noticed his wonder at the apparent size and ferociousness of the dinosaurs. "Let's go see some of these animals," said the tutor. They went to the local natural-history museum, whereupon the child began to talk about how he would fight dinosaurs if he found any real ones. That incident led to the tutor's recording a story that the boy dictated, and they used it as a beginning for learning words and for becoming interested in the relation of spoken words and printed symbols. Parents need to look for similar opportunities to spark their children's interest.

Materials

This book has described many activities and offered numerous exercises that you can use with your child. Likewise, extensive booklists give you many choices of reading materials to work with and enjoy. If you find that your child is having any particular problems with school work, you may wish to examine his or her classroom books and see if there are ways to work directly with these materials. To add variety to the reading materials that you use in the home, you can break away from educational materials and books sometimes and utilize newspapers and magazines. You should feel free to work with whatever is readily available to you and whatever keeps your child interested in learning.

Newspapers and magazines

These periodicals are always available, are inexpensive, and appeal to a wide variety of interests. Try some of the following suggestions for using them to promote your child's reading and learning skills.

➡ **Headlines.** Headlines from newspapers and article titles from magazines can be used to teach children to think about the content of articles. Word-analysis skills can also be developed from headlines. Headlines are in bold type and can easily be cut up for word-recognition activities and various kinds of language games. Try having your child put together cut out words to make sensible statements.

"Europe Split on Election": What does this headline mean? What do you expect to find in the article? Depending on the background and age of the child, he may be able to infer what will be in the article. But he may need assistance in seeing how headlines give the reader clues to the contents. Point out that the head enables him to form questions that will guide his reading.

What is Europe, and what is an election, or what election is referred to? Only with that kind of knowledge can the learner make sense from the headlines and prepare himself to read the article. Then he can ask why Europe is "split."

Take the head "U.S. to Leave Middle East in Five Years." Does the reader know what the "Middle East" refers to? Does that head indicate a promise? Is it something that is hopeful, or is it a doleful comment? The headline game is exciting. It calls for the reader to supply information, because the headline usually doesn't make a complete sentence. It sets up questions for reading. It enables you to check the child's comprehension by having him read an article and then select from several heads the one that best fits the article. It also enables you to get some notion of his background for reading and the level on which you can discuss things.

Headlines make reading something related to real life. What the newspaper is talking about relates to everyday happenings, sports heroes, the weather, war, crime, and movies. Reading becomes a vital activity.

CONGRESS GIRDING FOR LAME-DUCK SESSION

A child would have to have considerable experience to get the implication of that headline. It is loaded with images and words that are not common. How could you make it more meaningful? Have the child pantomime a lame duck. The term "girding" goes back to the Middle Ages when warriors girded themselves with armor in preparation for battle. What has all that to do with Congress? Why are lawmakers "crippled"? Certainly, the newspapers and magazines have many items that provide interesting comprehension activities, and they often can give the child material he can handle. The sports page is a good place to start many children. Common sports words can be cut from heads, and the child can underline those words as he finds them in articles. It is like a game that teaches him to recognize words, and shows how those words fit in a larger unit of meaning.

➥ **The comics.** Another easy reading activity is the comic page. The pictures enable you to develop the idea of a story, or a punch line, or the relation between text and illustration. All of these are helpful for reading textbooks. Once again you are helping your child read where it counts in his daily life. Comics are of high interest to children and adults and can be fun, even for a reluctant reader.

➡ **Table of contents.** By using a large newspaper such as *The New York Times,* you can demonstrate an important study skill with many reading applications. Ask your child to find an article on gardening in the newspaper, for example. Or, if you use a local paper, ask her to find out what is showing at the local movie theater. Typically, she will begin searching page by page or at random, not realizing that the newspaper has a table of contents. Here is an opportunity to teach her what a table of contents is, where to look for it, and how to use it. Magazines, including children's magazines, also have tables of contents and can be used to teach about this important location tool.

➡ **TV viewing schedules.** What TV programs are on Friday at 8:00 p.m.? Your child can learn to read charts by practicing with the schedules in *TV Guide* or in your local paper. In order to answer the question above, your child has to locate Friday's schedule, search the column for the correct hour, and then read off the list. This skill can be practiced casually as the family plans what programs to watch for the evening or the week. Or a game can be made of it. Your child can hunt for key words or phrases, such as "game" or "Movie of the Week."

If your child seems unable to work with the *TV Guide* at first, ask him if he would like to set that as one of his goals. Then say, "In two weeks we will make you a master at reading the *TV Guide.*" Run through a couple of quick exercises each night and test him at the end of two weeks to show his progress.

To read the *TV Guide* he had to learn to respond quickly to the words, to be able to skim over them without hesitation in order to answer the questions. He learned he had to cue himself to key features of the words and to use cues so he could answer your questions. Make it a game, and he will soon be asking for more of the same.

You can easily move from the *TV Guide* to other charts or maps. The same principle applies. Locate symbols first on the vertical and horizontal coordinates to locate places. This is a way to get children started on an important skill by taking advantage of high interest material.

➥ **Using pictures.** Pictures can be assets in helping a child comprehend. Pictures give the child a concrete image that will help to determine what an article is about. What if the following title appeared in a magazine without pictures: "The Opossum—A Special Kind of Animal"? For the child who has not seen an opossum or its picture, the animal could look like anything from a centipede to a jellyfish, with unlimited size variations.

But a look at the title along with a picture not only satisfies the child's curiosity about appearance but also supplies a whole new source of before-reading questions.

Ask the child, "What do you think this story is going to tell us? What's unusual about the animal? Look at this long tail. What other animal that you know does it remind you of? Why is the animal shown with a moon behind it and its young on its back? Use your imagination. What do you think this story might be about, judging from the picture?" In those few statements and questions you have focused the child's attention and asked him to associate the opossum with something already known, perhaps a squirrel. You have also created interest in the story or article and set some purposes for reading.

➥ **Magazine ads.** Magazine ads make great reading exercises. Usually there are illustrations and related copy. You can discuss an ad with your child without his realizing you are teaching him about reading. Look at an ad for a battery. Ask, "What does it stand for?" His awareness, for instance, of the Ford trademark may indicate an alertness about autos or about ads that appear in magazines and on television. You can use the headline to prepare for reading the ad. "What does the headline suggest? Now, read the ad, and we'll figure out the difficult words together."

Advertisements also offer exercises in critical reading. The purpose of an ad is to convince you to buy something or to develop a certain attitude about something. To accomplish this many styles and tactics are used. Ads can be subtle or bold, humorous, informational, philosophical, sentimental, and even deceptive. Identifying the tactics of an advertiser is a good reading exercise for anyone. It can be interesting and informative to both parent and child. Here is an example outside of school where you as a parent can demonstrate that the ability to read and read intelligently is of practical value.

Comments you make about ads when you are looking at them with your child could be like these:

"This hamburger ad is funny. It makes us remember and feel good about this restaurant. But does this mean they have the best hamburgers? Is this the kind of food we should eat?"

"This scenic picture of nature in the oil company ad is lovely. Why do you think they are using a picture like this? What kind of message is this ad trying to get across?"

"Why do you think this long-distance phone company ad tells us a story about old friends?"

Judging your success

Judging success in education is not simple, but here are some guidelines:

- After a lesson, is your child able to do something he wasn't able to do before?
- Your child ought to give some indication that he has a feeling of success. An important goal of working with your child is to create that feeling. Does he give you the impression that he is aware of his progress?
- Did you encourage her or praise her often for her effort during the lesson?
- Did you provide learning in small steps?

If you can answer yes to those questions, the chances are you succeeded in the lesson. There are degrees of success, and you will judge those for yourself as your experience increases.

Get started with confidence

Tips for reading and working with youngsters who need help are endless. You now have sufficient knowledge to begin with confidence. If you need or want additional knowledge, there are books suggested in the appendix that can help. The key point is that you can make an important contribution to your child's skills and to his life by encouraging him and guiding him through some simple practices. You are not expected to be the expert, and that is your strength in your relationship with your child. You are a coach and a cheerleader who says:

- Keep your eye on the ball.
- Let's practice together.
- Good job! You're improving all the time.

You are a friendly guide helping your child to succeed.

Appendices

The children's books listed in these appendices can be found in libraries and in bookstores. They are listed here by author and title, but full publisher order information is available in *Books in Print*, which is available at libraries and bookstores.

Appendix A —*Preschool Books*

Very young children enjoy hearing and looking at the pictures in these stories.

Ahlberg, Janet and Allan. *The Baby's Catalogue.*
Bang, Molly. *Ten, Nine, Eight.*
Barton, Byron. *Airport.*
Brooke, Leslie. *Ring O'Roses.*
Brown, Margaret Wise. *Goodnight Moon.*
———. *The Important Book.*
———. *The Runaway Bunny.*
Buckley, Helen Elizabeth. *Grandfather and I.*
Burningham, John. *Mr. Gumpy's Outing.*
Burton, Virginia Lee. *Mike Mulligan and His Steam Shovel.*
Carle, Eric. *The Very Hungry Catepillar.*
Chorao, Kay. *The Baby's Bedtime Book.*
Cohen, Miriam. *Will I Have a Friend.*
deAngeli, Marguerite. *Book of Nursery and Mother Goose Rhymes.*

Ehrlich, Amy. *Zeek Silver Moon.*
Ets, Marie Hall. *Just Me.*
Feelings, Muriel. *Jambo Means Hello: Swahili Alphabet Book.*
Flack, Marjorie. *Angus and the Ducks.*
Freeman, Don. *Corduroy.*
Gag, Wanda. *Millions of Cats.*
Galdone, Paul. *The Gingerbread Boy.*
———. *The Three Bears.*
Grimm Brothers. *The Shoemaker and the Elves.*
Hoban, Russell. *Bedtime for Frances.*
———. *Best Friends for Frances.*
Hoban, Tana. *Count and See.*
———. *Push Pull, Empty Full.*
Hurd, Edith Thacker. *The Mother Whale.*
Hutchins, Pat. *Rosie's Walk.*
Isadora, Rachel. *I Hear.*
Isadora, Rachel. *I See.*
Jonas, Ann. *Holes and Peeks.*
Jones, Rebecca C. *The Biggest, Meanest, Ugliest Dog in the Whole Wide World.*
Keats, Ezra Jack. *Peter's Chair.*
———. *Regards to the Man in the Moon.*
———. *The Snowy Day.*
Krauss, Ruth. *The Bundle Book.*
———. *The Carrott Seed.*
Kunhardt, Dorothy. *Pat the Bunny.*
Leaf, Munro. *Ferdinand.*
Lexau, Joan M. *Benjie.*
———. *Every Day a Dragon.*
Long, Earlene. *Gone Fishing.*
Maestro, Betsy and Guillio. *Traffic: A Book of Opposites.*
Massie, Diane Redfield. *Dazzle.*
———. *Walter Was a Frog.*
Mayer, Mercer. *Frog Goes to Dinner.*
McDermott, Gerald. *Arrow to the Sun.*
Minarik, Else Holmelund. *Little Bear.*
Munari, Bruno. *Munari's ABC.*

Numeroff, Laura. *If You Give a Mouse a Cookie.*
Parish, Peggy. *I Can—Can You?*
Piper, Watty. *The Little Engine that Could.*
———. *Mother Goose: A Treasury of Best Loved Rhymes.*
Potter, Beatrix. *The Tale of Peter Rabbit.*
Preston, Edna Mitchell. *The Temper Tantrum Book.*
Showers, Paul. *The Listening Walk.*
Singer, Isaac Bashevis. *Why Noah Chose the Dove.*
Skorpen, Liesel Moak. *Charles.*
Spier, Peter. *Crash! Bang! Boom!*
Tafuri, Nancy. *Have You Seen My Duckling?*
Tresselt, Alvin R. *It's Time Now!*
Udry, Janice M. *A Tree Is Nice.*
Waber, Bernard. *Lyle Finds His Mother.*
Watson, Clyde. *Father Fox's Pennyrhymes.*
Wells, Rosemary. *Benjamin and Tulip.*
Wezel, Peter. *The Good Bird.*
Williams, Garth. *Baby Farm Animals.*
Williams, Vera B. *A Chair for My Mother.*
Winter, Jeanette. *Hush Little Baby.*
Wright, Blanch Fisher, Illustrator. *The Real Mother Goose.*
Yolen, Jane. *Owl Moon.*
Zolotow, Charlotte. *William's Doll.*

Appendix B —Predictable Books

Predictable books contain patterns of language and patterns of plot that enable children to participate quickly in the act of reading. After hearing a predictable book once or twice a young child can pick it up and revisit it alone.

Aliki. *Go Tell Aunt Rhody.*
———. *Hush Little Baby.*
Asch, Frank. *Monkey Face.*
Beckman, Kaj. *Lisa Cannot Sleep.*
Blake, Quentin. *Mr. Magnolia.*
Bonne, Rose and Alan Mills. *I Know an Old Lady.*
Brandenberg, Franz. *I Once Knew a Man.*
Brown, Margaret Wise. *Four Fur Feet.*
———. *Home for a Bunny.*
Carle, Eric. *The Grouchy Ladybug.*
Carlstrom, Nancy White. *Jesse Bear, What Will You Wear?*
Charlip, Remy. *Fortunately.*
Cook, Bernadine. *The Little Fish that Got Away.*
Delaney A. *The Gunnywolf.*
deRegniers, Beatrice Schenk. *Willie O'Dwyer Jumped in the Fire.*
Duff, Maggie. *Jonny and His Drum.*
Emberley, Barbara. *Simon's Song.*
Ets, Marie Hall. *Elephant in a Well.*
Flack, Marjorie. *Ask Mister Bear.*
Galdone, Paul. *The Little Red Hen.*
Hoffman, Hilde. *The Green Grass Grows All Around.*
Hutchins, Pat. *Rosie's Walk.*
Ivimey, John. *Three Blind Mice.*
Keats, Ezra Jack. *Over in the Meadow.*
Klein, Lenore. *Brave Daniel.*
Koontz, Robin. *This Old Man: The Counting Song.*

Langstaff, John. *Oh, A-Hunting We Will Go.*
————. *Frog Went A-Courtin'.*
Laurence, Esther. *We're Off to Catch a Dragon.*
Lobel, Anita. *King Rooster, Queen Hen.*
Mack, Stan. *10 Bears in My Bed.*
Martin, Bill. *Fire! Fire! Said Mrs. McGuire.*
Mayer, Mercer. *Just for You.*
Memling, Carl. *Ten Little Animals.*
Neitzel, Shirley. *The Jacket I Wear in the Snow.*
    Illustrated by Nancy Winslow Parker.
Peppe, Rodney. *The House that Jack Built.*
Quackenbush, Robert. *Skip to My Lou.*
Raffi. *Five Little Ducks.*
Robart, Rose. *The Cake That Mack Ate.*
Scheer, Julian and Marvin Bileck. *Rain Makes Applesauce.*
Sendak, Maurice. *Where the Wild Things Are.*
Shulevitz, Uri. *One Monday Morning.*
Stevens, Harry. *Fat Mouse.*
The Tomten. Adapted by Astrid Lindren.
Vipont, Elfrida. *The Elephant and the Bad Boy.*
Wadsworth, Olive. *Over in the Meadow.*
Welber, Robert. *Goodbye, Hello.*
Williams, Linda. *The Little Old Lady Who Was Not Afraid of Anything.*
Zelinsky, Paul. *The Wheels on the Bus.*
Zolotow, Charlotte. *Do You Know What I'll Do?*

Appendix C —*Books on Audio Tape*

Books on audio tape can be used as read-along books in order to build fluency, or they can be used as stories to listen to, for example, while riding in a car. The notations after each title indicate the type of story and the awards it has won.

Grades K—3

Aardema, Verna. *Oh, Kojo! How Could You! an Ashanti Tale.* Random House-Miller Brody.
(folk tale — African)
————. *Why Mosquitoes Buzz in People's Ears.* Educational Record Center.
(folk tale) [Parents' Choice]
Aliki. *Digging Up Dinosaurs.* Listening Library.
(science) [Reading Rainbow]
Andersen, Hans Christian. *Thumbelina.* Rabbit Ears Productions.
(fairy tale) [ALA notable]
Anderson, John. *Pecos Bill.* Windham Hill.
(legend — American)
Chase, Richard. *Jack tales: More than a Beanstalk.* Educational Record Center.
(folk tale — American) [ALA notable]
Dahl, Roald. *Enormous Crocodile.* Caedmon.
(folk tale; animals)
Howe, James. *Howliday Inn.* Caedmon.
(mystery)
Keats, Ezra Jack. *Hi, Cat!* Live Oak Media.
(cats)
Kellogg, Steven. *Chicken Little.* Mulberry.
(animals)
Kipling, Rudyard. *The Jungle Books.* Recorded Books.
(folk tales)
Kipling, Rudyard. *Just So Stories.* Recorded Books.
(folk tales) [ALA Notable]

Kuskin, Karla. *Jerusalem Shining Still.* Caedmon.
(history) [ALA notable]
Lord, Jack. *Giant Jam Sandwich.* Houghton Mifflin.
(stories in rhyme; insects)
Marshall, Edward. *Three by the Sea.* Listening
Library.
(storytelling)
Milnes, Gerald. *Granny Will Your Dog Bite and Other
Mountain Rhymes.* Random House.
(rhymes) [ALA notable]
Prelutsky, Jack. *New Kid on the Block.* Listening
Library.
(poetry) [ALA Notable; Parents' Choice]
Rylant, Cynthia. *Henry and Mudge in Sparkle Days.*
American School Publishers.
(dogs; winter) [ALA notable]
Sharmat, Marjorie. *Nate the Great.* Listening Library.
(mystery) [Reading Rainbow]
Steptoe, John. *Mufaro's Beautiful Daughter.* Weston
Woods.
(folk tales — African)
Van Leeuwen, Jean. *Amanda Pig and Her Big Brother
Oliver.* Listening Library.
(humor; sibling rivalry)
Willard, Nancy. *Nightgown of the Sullen Moon.*
Random House-Miller Brody.
(fantasy)
Williams, Vera. *A Chair for My Mother.* Mulberry.
(family life; survival)
Wood, Audrey. *Heckedy Pig.* American School
Publishers.
(animals) [ALA notable]
Yolen, Jane. *Owl Moon.* Weston Woods.
(nature; owls) [ALA notable]
———. *Piggins.* Educational Record Center.
(mystery) [Parents' Choice]
Yorinks, Al. *In Coal Country.* Amerian School
Publishers.
(coal mining; occupations) [ALA notable]

Grades 4—6

Adams, Richard. *Watership Down.* Mind's Eye.
(animals; survival; environment)

Aiken, Joan. *Wolves of Willoughby Chase.* Bantam
Audio.
(Victorian drama) [ALA notable]

Baum, Frank L. *Wizard of Oz.* Recorded Books.
(fantasy)

Bryan, Ashley. *Dancing Granny.* Educational Record
Center.
(folk tale — African) [ALA notable]

Burnett, Frances Dodgeson. *Secret Garden.* Spoken
Arts.
(fantasy)

Burnford, Shelia. *Bel Ria.* Recorded Books.
(animals; historical fiction)

Carroll, Lewis. *Alice's Adventures in Wonderland.*
Recorded Books.
(fantasy)

Cleary, Beverly. *Dear Mr. Henshaw.* Random House-
Miller Brody.
(divorce; moving) [Newbery]

Cooper, Susan. *Silver Cow.* Weston Woods.
(fantasy)

Dodge, Mary M. *Hans Brinker: or, the Silver Skates.*
Caedmon.
(drama; family life)

Frost, Robert. *Swinger of Birches.* Educational
Record Center.
(poetry) [Parents' Choice]

Gipson, Fred. *Old Yeller.* Random House-Miller
Brody.
(dogs; historical fiction) [Newbery]

Gluskable Stories. Yellow Moon Press.
(folk tale — American Indian)

Grahame, Kenneth. *TheWind in the Willows.*
Recorded Books.
(animals; adventure)

Irving, Washington. *Rip Van Winkle and the Legend of Sleepy Hollow.* Recorded Books. (fantasy)

Jakes, John. *Susanna of the Alamo; a True Story.* Listening Library. (history)

Konigsburg, E. L. *From the Mixed-up Files of Mrs. Basil E. Frankweiler.* Random House-Miller Brody. (mystery)

Lewis, C. S. *The Horse and His Boy.* (Chronicle of Narnia, book 5) Caedmon. (fantasy)

McCaffrey, Anne. *Dragonsongs.* Performing Arts. (music; fantasy)

McKinley, Robin. *The Hero and the Crown.* Random House-Miller Brody. (fantasy; heroine) [Newbery]

Montgomery, L.M. *Anne of Green Gables.* Audio Book Contractors. (historical fiction; rural life)

Nesbit, E. *Railway Chidren.* Audio Book Contractors. (country life)

O'Brien, Robert C. *Mrs. Frisby and the Rats of NIMH.* Random House-Miller Brody. (fantasy; loyalty) [Newbery]

Peyton, K.M. *Going Home.* Audio Books. (family problems; runaways)

Rawls, Wilson. *Where the Red Fern Grows.* Bantam Audio. (dogs) [ALA notable]

Sewell, Anna. *Black Beauty.* Recorded Books. (animals)

Speare, Elizabeth George. *Sign of the Beaver.* Random House-Miller Brody. (historical fiction; Indians) [Newbery]

Stevenson, Robert Louis. *Treasure Island.* Cover-to-Cover. (adventure)

Appendix D —*Sample First Grade Reading Vocabulary*

This list was compiled from a study of six first-grade reading textbooks. If a word was used in at least three of the books, it is included in this list.

a	bakery	boys	come
about	ball	break	comes
act	balls	breakfast	coming
after	bandage	bus	cook
afternoon	baseball	but	cooked
again	basket	by	cooks
all	be		copy
alone	bear	cage	could
always	became	call	couldn't
am	bed	called	country
an	beds	calls	crack
and	beets	came	cracked
animal	began	can	crayons
animals	being	cans	cream
another	below	can't	cried
any	big	car	cry
anything	bike	care	cut
are	bikes	carrier	
around	bird	castle	dance
as	bird's	cat	danced
ask	birds	catch	dancing
asked	birthday	children	day
asks	bleeding	city	days
at	blooming	cleaned	did
ate	blue	cleaning	didn't
away	boat	clown	dime
awful	boo	coat	disgusted
	book	coats	do
baby	books	cold	does
back	box	color	dog
bad	boy	colors	dogs

doing	foot	hat	is
donkey	for	hate	isn't
don't	forgot	hats	it
door	found	have	its
down	four	he	
drive	friend	head	jump
drove	friends	hear	jumped
	frog	help	jumps
each	frog's	helped	just
eat	frogs	helper	
eating	from	helper's	kicked
eats	fun	her	kinds
egg	funny	here	king
eggs		hide	king's
elves	game	high	kitchen
end	garbage	hill	kitten
every	gave	him	kittens
everyone	get	himself	know
everywhere	girl	his	knows
	girls	holds	
fall	give	home	lake
family	gives	horse	last
fast	go	hot	laughed
father	goes	house	leaf
feel	going	houses	leather
feeling	gone	how	leave
feels	good	hugged	leaves
feet	good-bye	hurt	let
find	got	hurts	let's
finds	Grandma		letter
finger	Grandpa	I	letters
fins	great	ice	lie
first	green	idea	lies
fish	ground	if	like
flew		I'll	liked
flower	had	I'm	likes
flowers	hands	important	line
fly	happy	in	lion
food	has	into	little

live	much	part	red
lived	must	party	ride
lives	my	pea	rides
lizard		peek	right
long	name	people	road
look	need	piano	rock
looked	needs	pick	room
looking	never	picture	run
looks	new	pictures	runny
lost	next	piggyback	runs
love	night	place	
loved	no	play	sad
lunch	nose	played	said
lunchroom	not	players	same
	now	playground	sang
made	nurse	playing	sat
mail	nurse's	ponies	saw
make		pony	say
makes	o'clock	pot	says
man	of	pound	scales
many	off	present	scary
map	old	presents	school
mark	on	prince	sea
marks	one	princes	see
marry	only	pushes	seen
may	opposite	put	sees
me	opposites	puts	sentences
mean	or		shadow
means	other	queen	she
mice	our	question	shoemaker
might	out	quiet	shoes
milk	over		shop
money		rain	sign
more	packed	rains	silly
morning	paint	rake	sing
mother	painted	ran	singing
mouse	paints	read	sister
move	paper	reads	sit
moved	park	real	sits

six
sleep
slowly
snowed
so
soft
some
someone
something
sometimes
song
soon
sorry
sound
sounds
soup
stay
stayed
still
stop
story
street
such
sure
surprise
swam
swim

table
tail
take
takes
teacher
tears
tell
tells
than
thank
that

that's
the
their
them
then
there
they
thing
things
think
thinking
thinks
this
thought
three
threw
time
tiny
tired
to
today
together
told
too
took
treatment
tree
trees
turtle
turtles
two

umbrella
uncle
under
until
up
us
use

very

wait
waited
walk
walked
walking
walks
want
wanted
wants
was
wasn't
watched
water
way
we
went
were
what
when
where
who
why
wide
wife
will
windows
winter
with
without
woman
won't
woods
word
words
work
worked
would

wouldn't
write

yell
yelled
yellow
yes
you
your

Appendix E—*Literary resources*

Book Clubs

If books are available to a child, he's more likely to develop the reading habit. When a child owns books, they're nearby when he is ready to read. The book clubs listed here can help you place books within easy reach of your child.

- **Books of My Very Own**, Book-of-the-Month Club, 485 Lexington Ave., New York, NY 10017 (for four age groups, from babies to ten-year-old readers)
- **Junior Library Guild**, 666 Fifth Ave., New York, NY 10103 (seven age groups, preschool through high school)
- **Kids' Club**, Walden Book Co., 201 High Ridge Rd., Dept 52, Stamford, CT 06904 (children up to age 12)
- **Parents Magazine's Read Aloud Book Club**, 685 Third Ave., New York, NY 10017 (ages 2–7)
- **Weekly Reader Children's Book Club**, Field Publications, 245 Long Hill Rd., Middletown, CT 06457 (ages 4–11)

The following companies have a number of book clubs for children.

- **Grolier Enterprises, Inc.**, Sherman Tpke., Danbury, CT 06816
  Beginning Readers' Program (ages 3–6)
  Disney's Wonderful World of Reading (ages 2–6)
- **Newbridge Communications, Inc.**, 333 E. 38 St., New York, NY 10016
  Children's Choice (ages 2–7)
  Early Start (ages 6 mos.–2 years)
  PreSchool Book Club (preschool–grade 2)
- **Scholastic Inc.**, 730 Broadway, New York, NY 10003

Arrow Book Club (grades 4–6)
Firefly Book Club (ages 0–5)
Lucky Book Club (grades 2–3)
See-Saw Book Club (grades K–1)
Teen Age Book Club (grades 7–12)

Newspapers and Magazines for Children

Newspapers and magazines for children can create and increase a child's interest in reading. Parents and relatives may consider giving subscriptions, which can be long-lasting and worthwhile gifts.

- *Boy's Life,* Boy Scouts of America, 1325 Walnut Hill Ln., Irving, TX 75015
- *Calliope* (ages 9–15)
  Cobblestone (ages 9–15)
  Faces (ages 9–15)
  30 Grove St., Peterborough, NH 03458
- *Chickadee* (nature, ages 3–9)
  OWL (science, ages 9–12)
  P.O. Box 11314, Des Moines, IA 50340
- *Creative Kids* (gifted, ages 8–14) P.O. Box 637, Holmes, PA 19043
- *Cricket* (ages 6–12)
  Ladybug (ages 2–7)
  P.O. Box 52961, Boulder, CO 80322
- *Highlights for Children,* (ages 2–12) P.O. Box 269, Columbus, OH 43272
- *National Geographic World,* P.O. Box 2330, Washington, DC 20036
- *Odyssey,* (space, ages 8–14) 21027 Crossroads Circle, P.O. Box 1612, Waukesha, WI 53187
- *Penny Power,* (consumers, ages 8–14) P.O. Box 54861, Boulder, CO 80322
- *Ranger Rick,* National Wildlife Federation, 8925 Leesburg Pike, Vienna, VA 22184
- *Scholastic Magazines,* 2931 E. McCarty St., P.O. Box 3710, Jefferson City, MO 65102

- *Sesame Street Magazine* (ages 2–6)
  Kid City (ages 6–10)
  3-2-1 Contact (ages 8–14)
  P.O. Box 53349, Boulder, CO 80322
- *Sports Illustrated for Kids*, (sports, ages 8–13) P.O.
  Box 830609, Birmingham, AL 35283
- *Stone Soup*, (art and literature by children, ages
  9–14) P.O. Box 83, Santa Cruz, CA 95063
- *Turtle Magazine for Preschool Kids* (ages 2–5)
  Humpty Dumpty's Magazine (ages 4–6)
  Children's Playmate Magazine (ages 6–8)
  Jack and Jill (ages 7–10)
  Child Life (ages 9–11)
  Children's Digest (preteen)
  P.O. Box 7133, Red Oak, IA 51591
- *Weekly Reader*, 4343 Equity Dr., Columbus, OH 43228

Parents' Resources
Reading aloud resources

Bank Street College of Education. *Books to Read Aloud with Children through Age 8.* Bank Street College, 1989.

Barton, Bob. *Tell Me Another: Storytelling and Reading Aloud at Home, at School, and in the Community.* Heinemann, 1986.

Bauer, Caroline Feller. *Celebrations: Read-Aloud Holiday and Theme Book Programs.* Wilson, 1985.

Bibliography of Books for Children, Association for Childhood Education International, 1989.

Carroll, Frances L. *Exciting, Funny, Scary, Short, Different, and Sad Books Kids Like about Animals, Science, Sports, Families, Songs, and Other Things.* ALA, 1984.

Cooperman, Paul. *Taking Books to Heart: How to Develop a Love of Reading in Your Child.* Institute of Reading Development, 1986.

Fontaine, Elizabeth L. *Reading Aloud to Your Child: A Parent's Guide.* R & E Publishers, 1985.

Freeman, Judy. *Books Kids Will Sit Still For: The Complete Read-Aloud Guide.* NY: Bowker, 1990.

Kimmel, Margaret Mary. *For Reading Out Loud! A Guide to Sharing Books with Children.* (2nd ed.) Delacorte, 1988.

Lamme, Lina L. *Growing Up Reading: Sharing with Your Children the Joys of Reading.* Acropolis Books, 1985.

Lipson, Eden Ross. *New York Times Parent's Guide to the Best Books for Children.* Times Books, 1988.

Oppenheim, Joanne. *Choosing Books for Kids: Choosing the Right Book for the Right Child at the Right Time.* Ballantine, 1986.

Russel, William F. *Classics to Read Aloud to Your Children.* Crown, 1984.

Taylor, Denny. *Family Storybook Reading.* Heinemann, 1986.

Trelease, Jim. *New Read-Aloud Handbook.* (2nd ed.) Penguin, 1989.

Selection aids for children's books

American Library Association (ALA).
Caldecott Medal Books
Newbery Medal Books
Notable Children's Books
These lists are available at public libraries.

Children's books 1911-1986: Favorite Children's Books from the Branch Collections of the New York Public Library. NYPL, 1986.

Children's Catalog.

Fisher, Margery Turner. *Margery Fisher Recommends Classics for Children and Young People.* Thimble Press, 1988.

Gillespie, John T. *Best Books for Children: Preschool through Grade 8.* (4th ed.) Bowker, 1990.

Huck, Charlotte S., et al. *Children's Literature in the Elementary School.* (4th Ed.) Holt, Rinehart and

Winston, 1987.

Larrick, Nancy. *A Parent's Guide to Children's Reading.* (5th ed.) Bantam, 1982.

Lipson, Eden. *Parent's Guide to the Best Books for Children.* New York Times Magazine, 1988.

National Council of Teachers of English. *Adventuring with Books.* (9th ed.) 1989.

Reed, Arthea J. S. *Comics to Classics: A Parent's Guide to Books for Teens and Preteens.* International Reading Association, 1988.

Sutherland, Zena (ed.). *The Best in Children's Books, 1979-1984.* University of Chicago, 1986.

Winkel, Lois. (ed.). *The Elementary School Library Collection.* Brodart, *1984.*

Periodicals with reviews of children's books

Booklist
Bulletin of the Center for Children's Books
Horn Book
Parents' Choice
School Library Journal

Selected bibliography

Bibliography of Books for Children, Wheaton, MD: Association for Childhood Education International, 1989.

Huck, Charlotte S., et al. *Children's Literature in the Elementary School.* 4th ed. New York: Holt, Rinehart and Winston, 1987.

Kimmel, Margaret Mary. *For Reading Out Loud! A Guide to Sharing Books with Children.* 2nd ed. New York: Delacorte, 1988.

Larrick, Nancy. *A Parent's Guide to Children's Reading.* 5th ed. New York: Bantam, 1982.

Lipson, Eden Ross. *New York Times Parent's Guide to the Best Books for Children.* New York: Times Books, 1988.

Parents' Choice. Parents' Choice Foundation, Box 185, Newton, MA.

Smith, Carl B. and Ronald Wardhaugh. *Series r.* New York: Macmillan Pub. Co. 1975.

Smith, Carl B., et al. *Teaching Reading in Secondary School Content Subjects: A Bookthinking Process.* New York: Holt, Rinehart and Winston, 1978.

Trelease, Jim. *New Read-Aloud Handbook.* 2nd ed. New York: Penguin, 1989.

Index

Parents' Notes

Books for Home and School

from Grayson Bernard Publishers

❖ *Grammar Handbook for Home and School*
   by Carl B. Smith, Ph.D.

   A quick reference with concise explanations of the basics of English grammar and punctuation. The perfect companion to *Intermediate Grammar.*

❖ *Intermediate Grammar: A Student's Resource Book*
   by Carl B. Smith, Ph.D.

   A student's grammatical lifesaver! Complete explanations and examples, plus a handy punctuation guide.

❖ *Elementary Grammar: A Child's Resource Book*
   by Carl B. Smith, Ph.D.

   A handy source of answers and explanations for young learners and their parents.

Create a success story with . . .

Smart Learning:
A Study Skills Guide
for Teens by William Christen
and Thomas Murphy

Learn to focus study time and energy for fantastic results the whole family will be proud of!

. . . and for parents:

The Successful Learner Series

❖ **The Curious Learner: Help Your Child Develop: Academic and Creative Skills** by Marjorie R. Simic, Melinda McClain, and Michael Shermis

Parents can help their children become curious, well-rounded learners and see the value in all academic and creative pursuits.

❖ **The Confident Learner: Help Your Child Succeed in School** by Marjorie R. Simic, Melinda McClain, and Michael Shermis

An easy-to-read, interesting guide for parents on raising a child who is ready and motivated to learn.

"This is an extremely useful and informative book, written by experienced advocates of parental involvement in education."
— *Library Journal*

❖ **Help Your Child Read and Succeed: A Parents' Guide** by Carl B. Smith, Ph.D.

Practical, caring advice with skill-building activities for parents and children from a leading expert in the field.

❖ **Expand Your Child's Vocabulary: A Twelve-Week Plan** by Carl B. Smith, Ph.D.

A dozen super strategies for vocabulary growth— because word power is part of success at all stages of life.

Find these valuable resources at your favorite bookstore, or use the order form on the next page to have these books sent directly to you.

Order Information

☎ To order by phone, call toll-free 1-800-925-7853 and use your VISA or MasterCard.

✉ To order books by mail, fill out the form below and send

Grayson Bernard Publishers
P. O. Box 5247, Dept. C2
Bloomington, IN 47407

Qty.	Title	Author	Unit Cost	Total
	Grammar Handbook	Smith, C.	$ 8.95	
	Intermediate Grammar	Smith, C.	$16.95	
	Elementary Grammar	Smith, C.	$13.95	
	Smart Learning	Christen/ Murphy	$10.95	
	The Curious Learner	Simic, M.	$ 9.95	
	The Confident Learner	Simic, M.	$ 9.95	
	Help Your Child Read and Succeed	Smith, C.	$12.95	
	Expand Your Child's Vocabulary	Smith, C.	$ 7.95	

Shipping & Handling
$3.00 for the first book plus $1.00 for each additional book.

Method of Payment
❑ check ❑ money order
❑ Master Card ❑ Visa

Subtotal	
Shipping & Handling	
IN residents add 5% sales tax	
TOTAL	

Card holder_____

Card no. _____

Expiration date _____

Send books to:
Name _____

Address _____

City_____State _____ Zip _____

Prices subject to change.

Your satisfaction is guaranteed.

Special Offer!

Write or call now for your free year's subscription to Grayson Bernard Publishers' parent newsletter:

Parent & *Child . . . learning together*

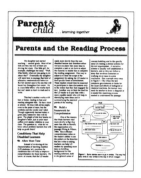

Receive four quarterly issues filled with information and advice all concerned parents need.

Simply mail in the order form below or call (800) 925-7853 for your free subscription.

Name _____

Address _____

City _____ Zip _____

Ages of my children _____

Topics I'd like to read about _____

Mail to: Grayson Bernard Publishers
Free Subscription Offer
P.O. Box 5247, Dept. RS2
Bloomington, IN 47407

Grayson Bernard Publishers is a publisher of books for families and educators dedicated to promoting literacy and educational achievement. Our primary goal is to provide quality resources for parents and children to enrich the home learning environment.

For more information about *Help Your Child Read and Succeed* or any of our publications, please contact us at:

Grayson Bernard Publishers
223 S. Pete Ellis Drive, Suite 12
P.O. Box 5247
Bloomington, IN 47407
(800) 925-7853